The Land of the Churnet

The visitor centre at Tittesworth Reservoir

Alan Gibson

Acknowledgements

For information about Whiston Hall and the Golf Club, my thanks to Richard Cliffe, Kath Harrison, Peggy Swinson and Mr G. Wood.
For the drawings and pictures added to the book by Sally Richardson.
To Staffordshire Historic Environmental Records Office and Suzy Blake

Recommended Reading

The Victoria County History, Staffordshire Vol II &Vol VII	
A Long Way from Home Reminiscences of the Polish Community	Ed. Sheena Barnes
Around Meerbrook	Sheila Hine
Quarries of Cauldon Lowe	Basil Jeuda
Rudyard Reflections	Basil Jeuda
Dieulacres Abbey	Michael Fisher
History of Leekfrith	Mary Breeze
History of Cheddleton	Ed. Robert Milner
Brittain's Paper Mills	Robert Milner
Miscellaneous Notes	J.D. Johnstone
The Wardle Story	Ann Jacques
Finding Susanna	Pam Inder & Marion Aldis
Swythamley	Sir Philip Brocklehurst
Staffordshire Legends	Alan Gibson
A History of Leek	Ray Poole
A History of Rocester	Alan Gibson
Cheddleton Memories: Bittersweet	Alan Gibson
History of Alton and Farley	Univ. of Keele & local residents
St Edward's Hospital	Max Chadwick & Dave Pearson
Thomas Bolton & Sons Ltd	John Morton
The Trent & Mersey Canal	Jean Lindsey
List of Buildings of Special Architectural & Historic Interest	Dept of Environment
The Iron Valley (Churnet Valley Iron)	Herbert Chester
Analysis & Formation of Upper Roches & Churnet Valley	M.R. Darke
Consall Forge	University of Keele
20th Century Foxt	Courtesy of Mrs C.M. Chester
Oakamoor Remembered	Peter L. Wilson
Pugin Land	Michael Fisher
A Vision of Splendour	Michael Fisher
Alton Towers: A Gothic Wonderland	Michael Fisher
Staffordshire Records Office	
William Salt Library	
Uttoxeter Library	

CHURNET VALLEY BOOKS
1 King Street, Leek, Staffordshire. ST13 5NW 01538 399033
www.leekbooks.co.uk
©Alan Gibson and Churnet Valley Books 2005
ISBN 1 904546 32 3

CONTENTS

Lime kiln Froghall.

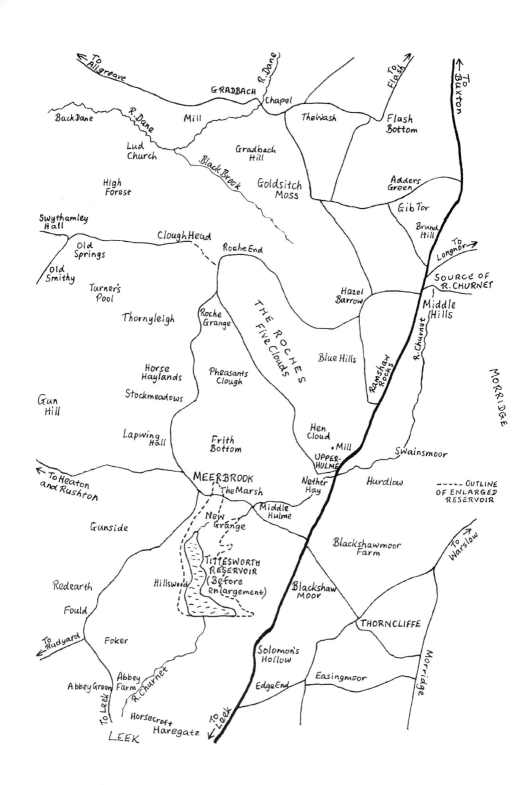

Introduction
The Land of the Churnet

The towns and villages along the course of the Churnet, from its source near Flash to its confluence with the Dove beyond Rocester, owe their settlement and their livelihoods to the river. The river provided not only water, it supplied the power and the drain for the industries that grew up along its relatively short course. From the dyeing and silk mills of Leekfrith and Leek, to the paper and flint mills of Cheddleton, to the metalworking of Froghall and Oakamoor, back to the cotton mills of Rocester, the river worked very hard through hundreds of years. Now increasingly it is returning to nature and the valley becomes more and more simply a place to live in or visit as the manufacturing age passes it by.

The source of the Churnet, if we simply start at its highest point, is just beyond Bareleg Hill, a few yards away from the junction of the Longnor and Buxton roads near the Royal Cottage and Flash. Less than a mile away another spring eases its way out of the peat at Strines, just above Merryton Low. The two merge above Upper Hulme and form the river that has played such an important part in the prosperity of the towns and villages of the Churnet Valley.

This high area has always been a hard place to live, with isolated farms or tiny hamlets eking out a living, keeping a few livestock and perhaps growing oats for their daily bread. Button-making, packhorses, small scale quarrying and mining were the main sources of money. There were few proper roads before the end of the 18th century, only winding paths or packhorse tracks.

The Industrial Revolution had a devastating effect on the Churnet. The river, in the 17th century, would have been as clean and pretty as the Coombes Brook. Grayling and trout would have graced its swift flowing waters. But nature, in a perverse way, was responsible for the working class nature of the riverside populations. The population benefited from the geological turmoil that had occurred long before the ice ages that formed the valleys. The flora and fauna that now make our valley so attractive, flourishes on the very minerals that generations worked hard to extract, and the fast flowing streams were an obvious source of power from the earliest days.

The geological layering is far from even in the area. Layers of ore can be found just below the surface, before disappearing to a depth that requires pit shafts and expertise. The Churnet Valley, especially in the areas around Consall and Oakamoor, was rich in deposits of iron ore, copper, limestone and coal, as well as smaller deposits of manganese. In general, the coal deposits were of poor quality. In places where the strata of sandstone or millstone grit would allow, the primitive foot-rail mines produced small volumes of coal whilst the deeper sinkings were prone to flooding. A few miles away, the superior quality of the carboniferous deposits brought about the greater prosperity of the Cheadle coalfields.

With the introduction of the canal system and the cutting of the Caldon canal, the extraction of minerals changed from small groups of individuals transporting ore by packhorse, to entrepreneurs who employed gangs of men to load ore and limestone onto barges for the industrial towns of the Midlands and beyond. Many businesses set up in the Churnet Valley, to reduce their transportation costs, and the mineral debris and the pollution from the factories, found its way into the Churnet.

The factories of Leek were putting the longstanding local knowledge of textiles to good use, with entrepreneurs quick to grasp the significance of mechanisation. The dyes used to colour the silks and ribbons ended up in the river and villages downstream were treated to a multitude of colours as toxic chemicals were simply washed away - out of sight and out of mind! River flora and fauna were either killed or much diminished and layers of silt built up, creating flooding and erosion. Fish life all but disappeared.

The Industrial Revolution saw the working man coming off the land and into the factories to earn more money. Social changes and improvements in education slowly followed, but the die was cast and the old order was gone forever. The men and women at the heart of the revolution demonstrated character and determination, and some went on to fame and fortune, others to obscurity. These industrial pioneers who lived and worked by the banks of the Churnet are an integral part of our story.

The story also encompasses the characters and tales along the way; and inevitably there is reference to the natural beauty along the river and the opportunities for recreation.

Towards the end of the 20th century came the realisation that industrial pollution had to be controlled and now in the early 21st century the effects of enforcement are evident. The Churnet is cleaner, fish are returning, wildlife flourishes and the scars of industry are slowly being healed over by nature itself. In 2005, millions of pounds have been spent by Severn Trent putting in large new sewers along the course of the Churnet in Leek with a new pumping station in Barnfields, taking the sewage on to the modern state of the art plant at Leekbrook. This will surely enhance the waters still further.

Chapter One
Flash to Leekfrith

THE HIGHLANDS OF STAFFORDSHIRE, LAND OF LEGENDS

This is the Highlands of Staffordshire, at times a quiet and lonely place. It is the land of legends and ghosts, in the past the dread of travellers, a bleak outpost of moorland and steep valleys, jagged rocks and fast flowing streams, where drizzle and low cloud restrict visibility to a few yards.

The village of Flash, reputed to be highest in England, is the subject of Judge Reugg's book about forgery and counterfeiting in the moorlands. 'Flash money' was a common name for forged notes and is said to have come from the association with the village. The stories often centre on the meeting of the three counties in the area - the Three Shire Heads - where miscreants could move easily from county to county, and the jurisdiction of different magistrates.

Judge Ruegg was a circuit judge in North Staffordshire who lived in Uttoxeter who wrote several books with a national appeal. His popular book, *Flash,* tells of the remoteness of the village which made it almost impossible to reach in poor weather and unmade roads and half hidden tracks known only to locals who had little regard for law and order. The stranger in the story won the confidence of the locals when he stayed in Longnor, but the moors and the Morridge winter were responsible for his death.

Famously, forgers were apprehended at Meg Lane, near Sutton, on the old Leek to Macclesfield road, and after standing trial at Chester assizes, the gang leaders were sentenced to death by hanging, while several others were deported to Australia. Another counterfeiting operation was centred at the Bottom House Inn on the Ashbourne road a few miles out of Leek. The Fearns family were eventually apprehended by Nadin, the assistant chief constable of Manchester, who was employed by the Bank of England specifically to reduce the amount of counterfeit notes abroad at the time. The Fearns were notorious counterfeiters with a nationwide network of dealers. Some years later, in Leek, a die used to make coins was found hidden in the brickwork of a house that was being knocked down to make way for road-widening.

The villagers of Flash pay scant regard to such tales nowadays. But many locals would have been familiar with the legends and ghosts that haunt the moorlands. The wandering Jew legend goes back to biblical times and is the subject of a well-known moorland story. In about 1650, there lived locally an

A Flash note.

The beacon at the Mermaid which
looks down upon the infant Churnet
and over to the Roches, and the
Cloud in Cheshire.

The length of the Roches
seen from Morridge.

old man who had been lame for as long as anyone could remember. He tried many cures but none were successful. One Sunday afternoon he heard a knock on the door and upon opening it, encountered a strangely clad man who enquired if he could partake of a cup of ale. The old man, ever hospitable, made the stranger welcome and joined him in a cup of local brew.

The stranger, noticing the old man's disability, asked him how long he had been lame. After telling his story, he was amazed when the stranger announced that he would cure him: *'Take two or three bay leaves steeped in ale, each night, for two or three weeks and you will be restored to full health. But, constantly and zealously serve God'*. The old man did as he was told and in a few weeks time began to improve until he gradually made a full recovery. When the old man told his neighbours about the stranger, it was agreed that it was the wandering Jew, destined to walk the earth for ever as a repentance for denying Jesus a cup of water at the time of his crucifixion.

Another legend, based in the Warslow area, tells of the headless-horseman who roamed the moorlands. There was once a mighty warrior who was decapitated in battle. So sudden was it that the warrior remained on his horse still clutching his studded staff, and his faithful horse returned with him to his moorland home. From that time the warrior's spirit never left the area and from time to time revealed itself to unsuspecting travellers.

One occasion involved a farmer who was returning home on foot from Leek, where he had enjoyed refreshment in some of the towns many public houses. As the night began to draw in he was relieved to see a rider approach who offered him a ride home. No sooner had he mounted than he realised, to his horror that he was sitting behind the Headless Horseman. Away they galloped at breakneck speed, clearing hedges and ditches in a single bound. In no time they arrived at the farmer's house where he was flung to the ground. The poor farmer, severely injured, crawled to his bed where he remained until death eventually brought an end to his suffering.

UPPER HULME

Upper Hulme was a medieval settlement and despite its small size it has been an industrial site for seven hundred years.

The number of farms in the immediate vicinity point to a long settled community. Broncott farm, standing close to the Back brook is recorded in 1299 as belonging to the widow of Henry de Broncott, and the lands relating to Broncott farm are still in use today. By 1327 the *'vill and lands of Broncott'* had passed to Ranulph of Bagnall. The estate remained in the care of the Bagnalls until 1432 when it was sold to Roger Fowells. The Fowells held the property until 1592 when they sold it to John Harper of Alstonefield manor.

To the north east of Upper Hulme stood Knowle farm, where Robert of Knolles is recorded as tenant in 1308 and, to the east stands Hurdlow farm, reputed to have belonged to the monks of Dieulacres abbey.

A house was built to the north of Broncott for a Joseph Billing, who was described as a stone cutter and no doubt worked at a local quarry - there were several in the Heathylee area. Joseph's house, in later years, became the New Inn which in turn became the Olde Rock public house.

The inns and farms would have provided lodgings for the local workforce engaged in stone quarrying, coal mining and button making. Two coal mines are recorded, both of which are close enough to have worked the same coal measure. A mine at Back brook, above Upper Hulme, was in use in 1401 when Richard Strongarme took out a lease on two mines and a forge. In the same year Thomas Smythe took out a lease on a vein of coal at nearby Black brook. In 1404 John Topless was also mining at Black brook and a Robert Hulme took out a twelve year lease in 1415.

The Blue Hills were the main source of coal deposits. A mine was being worked there in 1680. In 1764 Sir Henry Harpur was the landowner when he let a mine at Blue Hills to James and Tobias Mallors for twenty-one years. The rent was taken at a rate of 10% of the coal produced. By 1796 the ownership had passed to the Earl of Macclesfield and was referred to as the Blue Hills colliery. It was still in operation in 1869 when four miners are recorded as living in the area, but by 1881 only one miner is recorded.

Apart from mining, quarrying and farming the main source of income outside was from button making. This cottage industry was common throughout the moorlands and contributed to the reputation of Leek. One of the streams that gushed from the mines in the Blue Hills contained a rich source of mineral that turned the colour of the wooden buttons to a rich shade of black.

The New Inn was the base for the Colliers' Refuge Friendly Society formed in 1842 and it quickly built up a membership of 164. A brass band, formed in 1850, probably drew its membership from this Friendly Society.

The Methodists took a lively interest in the Upper Hulme area and the moorlands in general. They held meetings in the homes of its followers - by the late 1820s meetings were being held at the Ridge Head home of Isaac Billings and at Hole Carr and Upper Hulme. A chapel was built at Upper Hulme in 1837 and an evening congregation of thirty was recorded. The chapels also served as a source of education in the area. A school existed, as the title of schoolmistress occurs frequently in the gazetters of 1841, 1851, 1861 and 1881. Ramshaw school was built in 1884 when Sir John Harpur Crewe funded the cost of the building south of the Royal Cottage. The school survived until 1970.

Sleigh, in his *History of the Parish of Leek* refers to a Richard Caldwell of Overholm, '*The learned Richard Caldwell, doctor in Phisicke'* who was born at Overholm, circa 1513, and '*was educated at Brazenose College, Oxford, of which he became a fellow'*. He ultimately became president of the College of Physicians at London where, in conjunction with John Lord Lombley, he founded in 1582 a chirurgical lecture, with a liberal salary. He wrote several treaties on physicke and translated the *Table of Surgery* by Horatio Moro of Florence. He died in 1585 and was buried at St. Benets, near to Paul's Wharf.

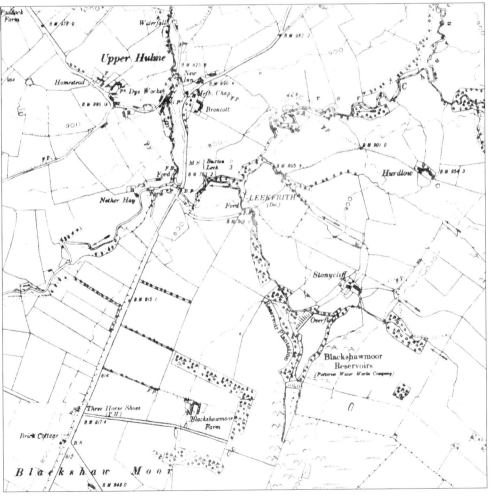

The Upper Churnet Valley, from an early 6" Ordnance Survey map.

The fire at Tatton's Mill, Upper Hulme, in 1891.

The workforce at Tatton's mills in the 1920s.

Dain's Mill.

The Roches stand guard over the Churnet Valley and Leek.

Blackshaw Moor camp was established for American forces in the build up to D-day.
After the war it became a refugee camp for the Polish - see further reading.

The waters above Upper Hulme were strong enough to power the early wheels of industry. In 1220, Ranulph, Earl of Chester granted to Dieulacres abbey a mill at Upper Hulme. It may have stood on Back brook as a mill was in use there at the Dissolution in 1538. The same mill may well have been in use more than a century later when it is recorded in 1670. Thomas Gent of Upper Hulme built a mill at Back brook in 1560, which evidently affected another mill nearby - a complaint in 1599 claimed Gent's mill was drawing water away from the Hulme mill and resulted in Gent's mill being demolished. William Gent, the grandson of Thomas, then let the site to John and William Hind who rebuilt the mill in 1602. In 1610 the mill was leased to Robert Deane and in later years became known as Dain's or Deane's mill. The mill survived until 1946, in later years run by Thomas Hine..

The Churnet continued to support various trades including silk throwing, flax spinning and dyeing. William Lowndes, a silk thrower, is recorded in 1824. In 1831 there was a four-storeyed silk mill, a house and four workers cottages in Upper Hulme. George Parker ran a mill employing eighteen workers and in 1860 John Beardmore was using the mill for spinning flax and dyeing. In 1869, William Tatton, a Leek silk dyer, purchased the mill and opened a dyeworks, and the firm, later as William Tatton & Sons, would operate here for 100 years. In 1891 a fire - always a risk in textiles - destroyed most of the mill but it was rebuilt and the business went from strength to strength. By 1924 the mill also wound rayon and in 1928 warping machines were in use. A new factory was built at Upper Hulme in 1931 but in the late 1940s the business was centred on modern premises in Buxton Road, Leek. Later, in 1969, the business was sold and the Upper Hulme site closed.

The mills were used by various other light industries thereafter and are still active in 2004, with an engineering company, a furniture making business and a dealer in fertilizers.

THE BROCKLEHURSTS OF SWYTHAMLEY

The Brocklehursts were local gentry who prospered as yeoman farmers and further extended their fortunes during the industrial revolution. J & T Brocklehurst of Macclesfield became one of the largest silk manufacturers in the country and John Brocklehurst was the Member of Parliament for Macclesfield from 1832 until 1868.

William Brocklehurst was the manager of the Brocklehurst Bank, and it was he who bought Swythamley Hall and its estate from the Trafford family in 1831. The de Traffords had held the estate since the time of the Dissolution in 1538, and before then it was part of the estates of Dieulacres Abbey. It would have been known as Swythamley Grange.

Philip Brocklehurst was adopted by his uncle and eventually inherited Swythamley Hall and the estate. He turned out to be an excellent landlord and administrator and the estate prospered under his tenure. Swythamley occupies a remote position, close to the Cheshire and Staffordshire border and it suffered from a lack of services. Sir Philip introduced a daily postal service, a savings bank and a money order office. He also improved the local roads, and concerts and tea-parties brought entertainment for the winter months. He died in 1904.

He had two sons, Philip and Courtney. Philip, also later Sir Philip, went on Shackleton's expedition to the South Pole in the *Nimrod* in 1908. Much of the finance for this famous exploration was provided by his mother the Dowager Lady Brocklehurst. He had a toe amputated through frostbite on the trip and this would remain in a bottle on the mantelpiece at Swythamley until he died. When he died there was still one of Shackleton's sledges in the outhouses. The Ship Inn at Wincle was named after the Nimrod as its sign shows to this day.

Courtney was not to be outdone by his older brother and was on board the *Endurance* in 1914 as it set off for Shackleton's second polar exploration. Unfortunately, at this moment, war was declared and all officers were recalled for service and Courtney had to return to the Dragoons and the First World War.

Courtney was responsible for the famous Roches wallabies. Between the wars he made a collection of wild animals, essentially a private zoo on the estate. At the outset of the Second World War, when he was again called upon to serve his country, the animals were allowed to roam the estate between Swythamley and the Roches. There were arctic foxes, deer and a yak - and wallabies. Most soon perished but a colony of wallabies managed to establish itself in the rocks and woods. The shy and elusive creatures continued to defy the odds for several generations and regular sightings excited tourist and walkers until somewhere around 2000 the last two females died. Courtney died at the hands of the Japanese while leading a company of soldiers through Burma.

It was the old Philip who cleared many of the old tracks and footpaths that give access to the Roches. He also organized the royal visit to Leek in 1872. Previous royal visits had not been so successful. Bonnie Prince Charlie had put the townsfolk in fear of their lives in 1745. And James I is reputed to have taken one look at the Roches and declared that Staffordshire was only fit to be cut into thongs to make highways for the rest of the kingdom.

H.R.H. Princess Mary of Cambridge (the future Queen to George V) and the Prince Teck thought differently. They had stayed with the Earl and Countess of Shrewsbury at Alton and word was passed to the authorities in Leek that their

Royal Highnesses would pass through Leek about noon, on Friday 23rd August. The occasion of their visit was to attend a picnic given by Mr Brocklehurst of Swythamley at his moorland shooting lodge. The place selected was Rock Hall, set among the wildest reaches of the Roches.

The whole town turned out to watch and to give the party a rousing moorlands welcome. About 1 o'clock the 'iron horse', a special train from Alton, consisting of a saloon carriage and three first class carriages, steamed into the station. A feu de joie was fired as they approached and the rifle band standing on the bridge played 'God Save the Queen'. Around 9,000 people packed the roads around the station as the royal procession set off. The route passed via Canal Street, into St Edward Street, on through Sheep Market, into the Market Place, where the crowd was so dense passage was almost impossible.

After their drive towards the Roches they were met by Philip Brocklehurst and Miss Brocklehurst, who escorted them on the more precipitous part of their journey to the picnic spot by Rock Hall. The picnic was a great success and the Earl of Shrewsbury proposed a toast to Mr Brocklehurst and Miss Brocklehurst.

The royal visit was Philip's finest hour and one of the occasions remembered by the people of Leek all their lives. The Brocklehurst name lives on although the estate was sold in the 1970s on young Sir Philip's death. His kindness and the good work of his father still endear them to the local people.

BEAUTIFUL TITTESWORTH

The road from Upper Hulme to Meerbrook affords a perfect view of the Leekfrith valley. The broad valley lies before you in all its splendour, the beautiful Tittesworth reservoir at its centre. Few would now object to its presence, although the original dam created by the Potteries Water Board in 1859 and the subsequent extension by Severn Trent Water Authority a hundred years later, brought about howls of local protest. Who could blame them? The flooding of the valley disrupted families who had farmed the area for generations, and these resolute and stoic characters were bred on adversity.

The weather can be very severe, the prevailing climate cold and wet, but on a fine spring day and in the height of summer, the spirit soon rises and you feel blessed with good fortune. The Roches stand sentinel, the heather blooms and you begin to understand just why the people of Meerbrook have such an affinity with the area. The Churnet Valley can boast many areas of natural beauty, but in its own special way, Leekfrith holds its own with the best - and the reservoir is now the jewel in the crown.

The Fountain Inn is gone as are the New Grange and other farms. The old school is now a youth hostel although it has been retained in its original state.

Swythamley Hall.

A carriage outside the hall.

New Grange farms seen before they were submerged beneath the newly enlarged Tittesworth reservoir in 1960.

Upper Hulme

Looking over Leekfrith and the beautiful Tittesworth Lake.

Buxton Road, Leek

The Methodist chapel is still in use as is the church, dedicated to St. Matthew. The Lazy Trout (the old Three Horseshoes) pub caters for visitors and locals alike, and the nearby Severn Trent Visitor Centre is very busy with walkers and visitors to the large children's play area and the fishing lodge.

The outskirts of the village is a host of ancient farms and smallholdings. Almost all are built from the local millstone grit that forms the southern end of the Pennine chain so evident in the Roches. Many of the farms are centuries old; some may well owe their existence to the monks of Dieulacres Abbey whose demesne lands once dominated the area.

That Meerbrook takes its name from the Meer brook is plain to see. There is a reference to Meer brook in c.1220 which relates nicely with the building of the abbey in c.1214. The name Frith indicates a wooded valley and the prime task of the monks and lay brothers would have been to clear the area of timber, thus increasing the amount of grazing land. Large flocks of sheep were introduced and the fleece used to produce the wool became a vital part of the abbey's income. Fulling mills were established on the Meer brook and the Churnet to clean and to enhance the quality of the wool.

The demesne lands, with their crops and flocks of sheep, were divided into granges and substantial farm houses were built to accommodate workers and equipment. Those not employed by the abbey settled into nearby hamlets and supported the area with their own trades and skills. Roche Grange and Wetwood Grange were among the first to be built and were in regular use by 1246. Another grange was built at Swythamley and yet another was built at Foker on the banks of the Churnet. Many of these buildings have long since disappeared along with the hamlets that sprung up in their shadows.

Henge Clud is now more familiar as Hen Cloud in the Roches. Overholm is now better known as Upper Hulme. Buxton Brow was once called Buckstone and is referred to as thus in one of the stories about Lud's Church. In 1340, woodland was recorded at Wetwood and Helliswood. Helliswood, now known as Hillswood, is a favourite walking place for Leek people.

More difficult to ascertain is the meaning of Sury, an area to the south of Abbey Green, where a bark house and a bark pit were in use in the early 16th century. The use of bark was common in the tanning industry but bark was also the common ingredient in the early manufacture of dyes. So the use of dyes in the vicinity of the Churnet may have been going on for a long time.

That a village or hamlet called Sury existed is not in dispute. Archival evidence records the marriage of a man from Sury to a woman from Meerbrook. Also recorded is the responsibility of the inhabitants of Sury to maintain the road that ran through the hamlet. The road was then part of an ancient coach road between Leek and Macclesfield. Adjacent to this road was a raised, cobbled pathway which may have been the route taken by the monks and their packhorses when transporting wool to Cheshire. A local colloquialism may have been responsible for a derivation of Sury - the monks' raised pathway became the only 'sure way' to reach the abbey when the Churnet was in flood.

Of more recent interest is the entry in Whites Gazetteer of 1834 which lists the local businesses of Leekfrith.

William Hammersley	Silk dyer,Whites Bridge
James Hulme	Wheelwright, Poolend
William Hulme	Day School, Meerbrook
Thomas Kerridge	Silk throwster, Upper Hulme

Inns & Taverns

Joseph Chappells	Abbey Green
John Abberley	Fountain, Upper Hulme
Saul Fisher	Three Horseshoes, Meerbrook
Charles Turner	Three Horseshoes, Blackshaw Moor

Blacksmiths

Charles Boyles	Meerbrook
Samuel Finney	Poolend
Thomas Rider	Poolend
Charles Turner	Poolend

Shoemakers

John Bratt	Meerbrook
John Brough	Middle Hulme
Abraham Hood	Upper Hulme

Twenty eight farmers and yeomen are also listed.

The gazetteer describes Leekfrith as an extensive township between two branches of the Churnet, *'comprising within its limits many scattered houses and the hamlets of Pool End, Whites Bridge, where there is a large dye house, Abbey Green, Meerbrook, Blackshaw Moor, and Upper Hulme. At the north end of the township are the moorland farms of Gunside, Rocheside and Haslewood.*

Meerbrook has a Chapel of Ease, which includes within its jurisdiction a great part of the township, and is dedicated to St. Matthew. It was built about 280 years ago by Sir Ralph Bagnall and is a curacy in the gift of the inhabitants and the vicar of Leek. The chapelry is exonerated from great tithes and the Earl of Macclesfield is Lord of the Manor, but a large portion of the soil belongs to John Brocklehurst and other freeholders.

The date given for the church varies. It seems likely that a chapel would have been in situ prior to the dissolution of the abbey in 1538 and the building of a new church would not have commenced until the dispute was settled. Ralph Bagnall may have authorised the building of the church in 1539 or later. Miller in his *Olde Leeke*, gives a date of 1565.

The village school closed in 1969 to end a period of education, much of it self-supported, of over 300 years. John Thomas, a schoolmaster from Leek taught in Meerbrook in 1623. John Comylach of Meerbrook is a schoolmaster in 1621. Ralph Poulson taught at Foker in 1662. Henry Royle is recorded as a schoolmaster in 1722 and continued to teach until his death in 1769.

Until 1778, the school was in a room in the church tower. The first village school was built shortly afterwards and a schoolmaster's house was added in 1839. The school was enlarged in 1871 and remained in use as an all age school until 1930. By 1940, it was the Meerbrook Church of England school and, with its 63 children, was designated a junior school. Further changes, in 1957, resulted in a change of name to St. Matthews Primary School.

Two Dame schools were supported by the village over the years offering a limited, scripture-led education to those too young for the church school or unable to afford the school pence. There were also the Sunday schools which reached their peak with that of Methodism in the 19th century.

The Methodists offered an alternative to the staid and class-ridden church of the 18th century. William Davenport of Fould farm was converted by the Quakers in 1654 and meetings at his house attracted up to thirty people. The house of John Cartwright of Upper Hulme was licensed for worship in 1693 for protestant dissenters. By 1862 Meerbrook and many moorland villages could boast their own non-conformist chapels.

Meerbrook 2000.

MISS ANN CLOWES

THE STAFFORDSHIRE POTTERIES WATERWORKS COMPANY

Plan referred to in Bill of Complaint

Taken from a plan produced about 1860 for Miss Ann Clowes, owner of the old Badnalls dyeworks on Mill Street, in her complaint against the Potteries Water Board over the pollution of the Churnet with muddy water.
Courtesy of Alan Bednall

DIEULACRES ABBEY

The Earls of Chester, great landowners in the 12th century, were generous benefactors to the religious cause. The abbey at Rocester can trace its beginnings to them, and Dieulacres also owes its existence to the Country's most influential landlord of the time.

Originally, an order of Cistercian monks was established at Poulton, on the banks of the River Dee a few miles south of Chester and founded by a local landowner, Robert Pincerna, in 1146, to pray for the health and safety of Ranulph, Earl of Chester.

The site at Poulton was not well chosen. For over sixty years the abbey was subject to attack by the marauding Welsh who frequently crossed the border and stole cattle and sheep belonging to the monks. The situation was brought to an end by the intervention of Ranulph de Blunderville, who decided that the abbey should relocate to a safer place. The place he chose was Cholpesdale, a broad, wooded valley, close to the town of Leek.

A more romantic version of the decision to move relates to a dream experienced by Ranulph. In the dream he was visited by the ghost of his grandfather, Ranulph I who instructed him to go to Cholpesdale and to there establish a community of Cistercian Monks where there had once been a chapel dedicated to the Virgin Mary. When the Earl awoke he told his wife about the dream. The Countess exclaimed 'Dieux l'encres' - May God grant its increase. And so the monastery moved from Poulton to Leek and the Cistercian abbey was built at Cholpesdale in 1214.

The abbey prospered to such an extent that in the course of time it became one of the wealthiest in the county. Its demesne lands stretched far beyond Leekfrith and at times bordered that of other monasteries as well as that of the

Dieulacres abbey ruins about 1890.

wealthy lords. Border disputes were not uncommon - the monastery at Croxden was in dispute with Dieulacres from time to time and a bitter feud with the Cheddleton family over the advowson of the church were but two of many.

The decision of the court in 1290 to grant the advowson to the Cheddleton family proved a bitter pill to swallow. Attempts to recover it caused a great deal of animosity. By the 1320s the dispute was at its height when William de Cheddleton and his followers went to Dieulacres and *'insulted and abused'* the Abbot until he was in fear of his life. William was described as a *'notorious disturber of the peace and a maintainer of false quarrels'*. His lifestyle was not untypical of the time when the wealthy took law and order into their own hands.

It seems, however, that the abbey prevailed for in 1345 William de Cheddleton granted to the abbot of Dieulacres all the rights to Cheddleton church and its lands. William's decision offered some justification to the abbot whose predecessors had held land in Cheddleton as long ago as 1240 when they built a bridge over the River Churnet and proposed a road leading to Cheddleton grange.

There can be no doubt that the wealth and power of the abbey would have allowed it to continue to prosper. It took a religious revolution, followed by the Act of Supremacy in 1534 to destroy it. Not only did Henry VIII procure the dubious rights to divorce his wives, he also laid claim to the riches of the Church of Rome invested in the monastic system.

The Court of Augmentation was quickly established with William Cavendish and Thomas Legh local auditors. All goods and assets were confiscated and disposed of and the buildings sold to the highest bidder

After the dissolution the site passed to the Earl of Derby and then via the Crown to Sir Ralph Bagnall. From Bagnall it eventually passed to the Rudyards and in the course of time was divided and passed through various families whose tenure was short-lived. The Rudyards are thought to have built the Abbey farm early in the 17th century but many of the other farm buildings, albeit modified, continued to be used for centuries afterwards. Much of the stone from the Abbey went into the old stone buildings of Leek.

BONNIE PRINCE CHARLIE & WILLIAM BILLINGE
At first sight it may appear to be stretching our story a little to place Charles Edward Stuart, the young pretender, in the vicinity of Leekfrith. However the roads that we are now so familiar with did not exist in 1745. The old road between Macclesfield and Leek passed well to the east of Gun and eventually reached the edge of Meerbrook before continuing by Gunside and Abbey Green. The Prince's route would have taken him towards Mill Street and then left and

up into the town, passing to the left of the church.

The stories of the highlanders feature in the Leek histories but what is not so well recorded is the story of William Billinge, born in 1679, died 1791 at the age of 112 years. His gravestone in Longnor churchyard records:

> In memory of William Billinge, who
> was born in a cornfield, at Fawfieldhead, in
> This Parish, in the year 1679. At the age of
> 23 years he enlisted into His Majesty's Service
> under Sir George Rooke and was at the taking
> of the Fortress of Gibraltar in 1704. He afterwards
> served under the Duke of Marlborough at
> the ever memorable Battle of Ramilles
> fought on the 23'd of May, 1706, where he
> was wounded by a musket shot in the thigh.
> He afterwards returned to his native country and,
> with manly courage defended his Sovereigns rights
> at the Rebellion in 1715 and 1745. He died within
> the space of 150 yards where he was born,
> and was interred here the 30th of
> January 1791, aged 112 years.
> Billeted by Death, I quartered here remain.
> When the trumpet sounds I'll rise and march again.

William was probably born into a farming family and his education would have been rudimentary at best. Children worked from an early age. But William was obviously healthy and lively and he escaped the humdrum of a moorland farm by enlisting in His Majesty's Services at the age of 23. William enlisted with Sir George Rooke the Commander of the Anglo-Dutch fleet and fought at Gibraltar. He later fought with Marlborough at the great battle of Ramilles where he was seriously wounded. It led to his eventual discharge but not before gaining great credit in several battles. I am indebted to John Forster MA, Education Officer at Blenheim, for these notes from their records:

'In this battle Billinge had the honour of being amongst the foremost of those few gallant soldiers who had the opportunity of rendering their commander very essential service by rescuing him from the most imminent danger; indeed, had it not been for those few brave men stepping in so opportunely his Grace must inevitably have been killed or taken prisoner; for, being thrown from his horse as he was leaping a ditch, the Marshal Villeroy, who both feared and admired the English General, was immediately informed of the Duke's disaster, and gave orders for some choice troops to hasten to the spot where the accident happened, and to bring the Duke dead or alive.

Billinge and his comrades, who had just time to throw themselves betwixt their commander and those sabub missionaries, played their part so well they scarce left one alive to carry the news to the Marshal. In this bloody conflict Billinge was severely wounded, a musket ball lodged in the thick part of his thigh, and in such part as to render any attempt to extract it quite impracticable; in this situation the ball remained thirty years, after which it made its way down the thigh, and came out at the ham. This `French Cherry' (as he always called the bullet) he carefully preserved until the day of his death.

The end of June the same year, Billinge had so far recovered from his wounds as to be able to assist in the opening of the trenches at the siege of Ostend, which place surrendered to the confederates on the sixth day of July. The conquest of this place opened such a scene of delight to Billinge, as he himself declared, that he never thought more of past dangers and that conquest and glory ought to be the only aim of a soldier.

He now began to think the more towns they sacked the more captives would fall to his lot. On 4th August Billinge was again employed at the opening of the trenches before Menir, one of the strongest fortifications in all Flanders being constructed under the immediate direction of that eminent engineer, Monsieur Vauban, who put his ingenuity to the stretch to render the fort impregnable, which surrendered the 22nd of the same month, after a bloody and obstinate resistance.

After his return to Longnor his reputation as a soldier would have made him a candidate to join the local militia whenever trouble brewed. He was indeed probably involved in putting down the Jacobite rebellion of 1715.

William's involvement with the rebellion of 1745, even though he would have been past sixty, is also likely. The Young Pretender led about 7,000 rebel troops from Carlisle to Derby, causing mayhem and fear along the way. His arrival in Leek caused chaos. The rebel soldiers, Scottish and French, were accompanied by a rabble of unkempt followers. All needed their food and keep. Leek made its excuses but paid dearly for the privilege of receiving Charles Stuart.

The irony is that Charles seemed to be unaware that all the towns between Derby and London were prepared either to support or not hinder his progress and in London the panic was so serious that a run on the pound threatened the Bank of England. Many people, commoners and gentry, were loathe to accept the Hanoverian King George - the Young Pretender offered a charismatic alternative. But instead of pressing on, Charles decided to turn back when his exhausted troops reached Derby. After a brief respite they marched once again towards Ashbourne and Leek and, ultimately, the Scottish borders.

And William Billinge still had over forty years to live!

Chapter Two
Leek and Lowe

EARLY DYEING AND INDUSTRY AROUND THE CHURNET

The Churnet forms the western boundary of Leek and Lowe. Entering the district at Broad's Bridge it flows along Mill Street before turning westward to form a wide loop around Leek, passing through White's Bridge on the Macclesfield road, to Westwood, Wallbridge, Birchall and Leekbrook. White's Bridge was once called Conyngre probably from 'coney', referring to rabbits. Rabbit was part of the staple diet and a rabbit warren almost certainly existed to the south east of Leek in the 13th century. At Westwood farm we find a reference to Cunney Greave and Rabbit Warren, and at Wallbridge farm, Rabbit Burrow.

Here on either side of the river local industry proliferated. The corn mill was one of two in the early 16th century, although the other, at Birchall, had been in existence for much longer - a mill was recorded there in the 12th century and in 1220 it was granted Dieulacres abbey by Ranulph, Earl of Chester.

The Leek mill was rebuilt in 1752 by the young James Brindley, the canal engineer, whose family had moved to Leek in 1726. Mill Street appears to have been a separate settlement on the edge of the town from the junction of Abbey Green road to Conyngre Bridge, now called White's Bridge. In fact it was part of the separate Parish of Lowe - Leek consisted of two parishes, Leek and Lowe. In the late 18th century there was a water-driven silk mill run by a Mr Sutton just downstream from Brindley's Mill. It later became Challinor's Dry Salt works, an important business providing the chemicals to the silk dyers.

The main road to Leek went via the present day Hencroft and on to Daisy Bank - an old cobbled lane is there today. By the 18th and 19th centuries the link with Leek would be more evident because of the new turnpike.

The Churnet was now becoming polluted and water supplies in Leek were also spasmodic and unhygienic with outbreaks of cholera. People were still using the river for drinking and washing alongside the dyers. Both were hit by the building of Tittesworth Reservoir in 1859 which led to muddy water.

There were many associated trades alongside the burgeoning silk and dyeing industry. In 1872, George Plant had a bobbin works on Mill Street that passed to Thomas Plant in 1890. The box making business of G.H. Plant & Son in 1940 was established in 1870.

Leek was also noted for its excellent ale - ale was the only safe thing to drink - and there were several small breweries in the town. Thomas Clowes, who kept the Pump Inn in Mill Street had a brewery on the junction of Canal Street (Broad Street) and Alsop Street. There was a brewery attached to the Blue Ball Inn in Mill Street in 1861 which was described as *'newly erected'* by Mr Marriot in 1865. Nearby, at Bridge End, a brewery was run by William Brown Lea in 1860. By 1864 it was run by Dixon and Jones. It was closed in 1866 when all of its stock, including beer and moveable assets, were put up for sale.

Near the Blue Ball was Mill Street Ragged School. Ragged schools were voluntary schools for poor children. The manufacturing and dyeing processes were labour intensive but the wages were very poor. The Ragged School opened in 1865 in a cottage in Belle Vue road. Demand was so great that within weeks the school moved to two adjoining houses in Mill Street. In 1866 the school was open on Sundays and for two hours every weekday evening. On Sundays reading was taught by twenty unpaid teachers to an attendance of eighty. At night school, pupils were taught writing and arithmetic and girls were also taught to sew. The Wesleyan Methodists agreed to take over in 1869 and the school was moved once again, this time to a newly built chapel that opened in 1871. In 1873 it became a public elementary day school known as the Mill Street Wesleyan School. It became an infant school in 1885 and remained so until it closed in 1913. The Ragged School name can still be seen above the entrance.

Most children leaving school were destined for the silk mills in the 19th century. Long hours and tiring work were the order of the day and the occasional strike did little to persuade the millowners to increase wage levels.

Edwardian Mill Street. The Ragged School is in the right foreground, with the Big Mill towering above the houses higher up the street.

Some found work in other trades but the wage levels were set by the silk industry. Leek, by now, was awash with silk and dyeing factories and the area between Abbey Green and White's Bridge was for many years occupied by the Churnet Works of Sir T & A Wardle, and the firm of Davenport Adams.

Other trades, noticeably engineering or agricultural based businesses also thrived, as first the canal and then the railways added impetus to the area. The firm of Woodhead and Carter in 1860 operated as millwrights and engineers close to the railway station. In 1872 the firm became Hope Foundry and was extended in 1886. Woodhead sold out in 1899 to J.P. Hitchcock, an iron and brass founder, and by 1908 it was known as the Churnet Valley Engineering Co. In 1912 it was Churnet Foundry. The Moorland Engineering Co occupied a site close to the canal wharf in the 1920s and closed in 1960.

THE BADNALL FAMILY, AN OLD SILK BUSINESS

Among the early pioneers who changed the silk weaving and dyeing business from a cottage industry to a mechanical factory system were the Badnall family. William Badnall was a dyer in 1725 and is referred to again in 1734, a dyer of mohair. William's dyehouse was on the corner of Mill Street and Abbey Green road. On the opposite side stood the linen thread works of Richard Ferne, who also owned a dyeworks on Ball Haye Brook. Shortly after 1736, Richard was declared bankrupt and his estate and his assets were purchased by William Badnall. By 1780 the business was being run by William's son Joseph.

Thomas Badnall is recorded as a silk dyer in 1790 and the factory is referred to again in 1809. By now the silk industry in Leek was gathering momentum and the first mill factories were about to change the face of local industry. In 1818, the Badnalls introduced steam power to drive what was described by a visitor at the time as a *'very modern factory'*. By this time they owned all of the land between White's Bridge and Abbey Green Road and had a virtual monopoly of the dyeing.

After Joseph died in 1803 the dyeworks were taken over by his sons, William and James Badnall. Another brother Richard, and his son, Joseph, later took over the business and formed a partnership with Henry Cruso and F.G. Spilsbury. The Badnall family were by now very wealthy and were financiers to many other businesses but there now occurred a 'run' on many of the 'country' banks in England. There were many bankruptcies and Richard Badnall was one of them. The partnership was dissolved in 1826 then continued by Joseph until his death in 1830. Richard was a bankrupt and for a period of time fled to the Isle of Man.

The business was now leased to John Clowes. When Clowes died in 1833,

Highfield Hall

Westwood Hall

Pickwood Hall

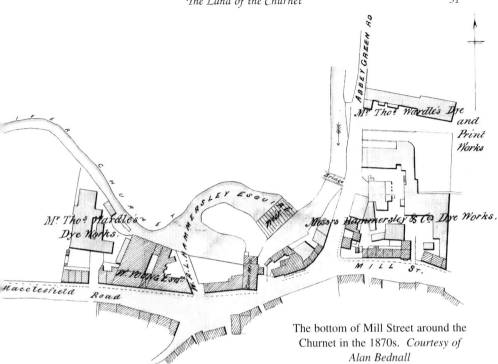

The bottom of Mill Street around the Churnet in the 1870s. *Courtesy of Alan Bednall*

it was leased to William Hammersley and this family ran the business successfully for many years with a silk dyeing works at Bridge End. The business was eventually taken over by Wardle & Davenport early in the 20th century.

Mary Badnall married John Cruso Senr, an important and wealthy solicitor - the Crusos are referred to elsewhere in relation to Foxlowe, the Cruso Association, and Pickwood Hall and the Challinors.

LEEK HALLS

Across the river, above White's Bridge, stood Highfield Hall, now the home of Leek Cricket Club. Highfield was an 18th century residence in its own grounds of 364 acres with two farms. The grounds have long been used for sporting activities: horse racing, athletics, bowls and archery are but a few. Edwin Glover, a wealthy Potteries' businessman moved there in 1870, when he purchased the estate from the Gaunt family. Glover continued the tradition of cricket at Highfield and was instrumental in it becoming the permanent home of Leek Cricket Club. When Glover died in 1886, Arthur Nicholson of Brough, Nicholson and Hall bought the estate (see later in chapter).

Also adjacent to the Churnet is Westwood Hall. Now one of Leek's two fine high schools, the hall was formerly a private residence that was much improved by John Davenport in the early 19th century. It was further extended in 1851 when a clock tower and a great hall were added. In 1868 it became the home of John Robinson until 1908 when it was purchased by the pottery manufacturer H.L. Johnson. In 1921 Staffordshire CC turned it into Westwood Hall Girls School which enjoyed an excellent reputation.

Westwood and Wallbridge are now a pleasant mix of fields and suburban housing but both bear traces of an historic past. A grange was built there in 1292, and old farms are recorded at Barnfields and Wallbridge.

Another grange was built by the monks at Birchall in 1246. At the time Birchall was described as a separate manor which in turn sub-divided into Big Birchall and Little Birchall. The Cheddleton road passes close to Little Birchall and in the nearby meadows a roman cinerary urn was discovered, giving rise to the idea that a Roman road once followed the route. The land between the road and the Churnet is now Birchall playing fields, the home of several local football teams. Leek Golf Club borders the route of the old canal and railway towards Sheephouse Farm. Sheephouse may have been in the demesne lands of Dieulacres abbey, and it was used as a tollgate in the 19th century.

The Red Lion in the Market Place was formerly Leek Old Hall. A half-timbered building, it was the home of the Jolliffe family in the early 18th century. They were wealthy wool traders and the house was the finest in the town. Later in the 18th century it became a coaching inn, and was the focus of activity in 1745 when Bonnie Prince Charlie's Scottish rebels passed through the town. The inn later played an important role in the social life of the town when its large function room was the scene of many grand occasions including the Leek Annual Ball. Many organisations used it as their meeting place.

Foxlowe is a fine Georgian house, built on an even older stone house at the north end of Leek Market Place and formerly the home of Mr and Mrs John Cruso. John Cruso was a solicitor, whose family firm were the successors to the Parker business. He was also from the Badnall family, silk manufacturers and bankers. Mrs Cruso was a great public benefactor and founded the Cruso Nursing Association, and the Cruso Aid in Sickness Fund provided relief in times of need to Leek silk workers.

At the end of the First World War Foxlowe served as a Red Cross Hospital for wounded soldiers. It later became a working mens' club and the headquarters of the Amalgamated Society of Textile Workers & Kindred Trades. The building had fine function rooms, the venue for many dances, and large gardens with a bowling green but in the 1990s changing times caught up with the union and the club. It is now being developed as an entertainment complex.

Haregate Hall was a substantial gentleman's residence in open countryside

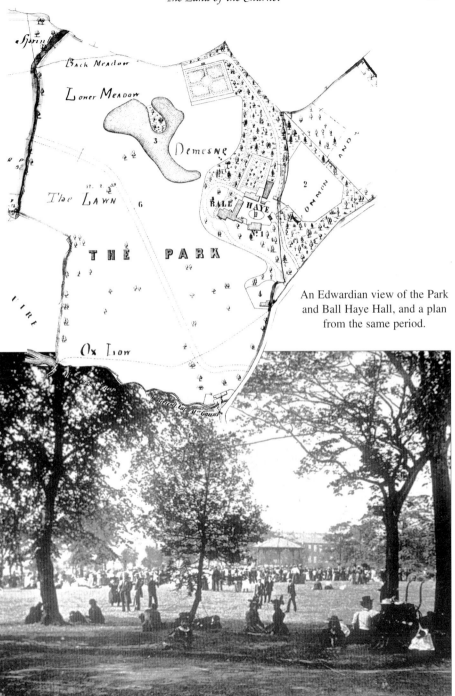

An Edwardian view of the Park and Ball Haye Hall, and a plan from the same period.

looking out to Tittesworth and the Roches. Its early history is bound up with the Toft-Chorley family of lawyers - a Toft is mentioned in connection with the march of Bonnie Prince Charlie through the Moorlands. It was the home of the Argles family in the 19th century but stood empty for many years as the result of death duties. Leek Urban Council acquired it in the inter-war years and the Haregate estate became the site of council housing during the 1950s - the 'Scheme'. The hall was converted to flats and is still there today.

Pickwood Hall is a large house in its own grounds between the Ashbourne and Cheddleton roads. It was the house of William Challinor, a solicitor by profession and a prominent citizen, serving as one of the Leek Improvement Commissioners. The business was his father's (originally Killminster and Challinor). In the 1850s William and his brother Joseph went into partnership with a Badnall who brought the interests of John Cruso, successor to the old Parker law firm, into the Challinors' Derby Street office. William Challinor achieved national recognition in the Law of Chancery and it is said that Charles Dickens acquired the theme of Bleak House from him.

Ball Haye Hall is fondly remembered by Leek folk. This grand house stood by the Park on the site of the present sports centre and its residents were prominent men in the silk industry. It was owned by the Brough family and later leased to John Hall of Brough, Nicholson & Hall. John was a generous man in the town and very active in the local scout movement. The Hall was acquired by the town between the wars, and during World War II it served as a base for American troops. It was demolished by the council in the 1960s. The park, gifted to the town by the Broughs, has always been known as Brough Park, and the area around the duck pond as John Hall's Gardens.

Woodcroft was another silk manufacturers' residence on the slope above Newcastle Road. In the 1880s it was the home of Henry Davenport and then William Prince who had a silk mill in Bath Street. The hall was demolished in the 1930s and is remembered in the name of Woodcroft.

LORD PARKER

In 1666 the block of stone property at the top of Leek Market Place between Foxlowe and the Vicarage was occupied by a Thomas Parker, and his son, also Thomas, was born there in 1666. He entered the legal profession and became an eminent barrister and Queen's Council. He served as Member of Parliament for Derby for many years and was knighted in 1705. In 1710 he became Lord Chief Justice, in 1716 he was created Baron of Macclesfield and in 1718 he became Lord Chancellor of England. He became Earl of Macclesfield in 1721.

During his career he earned himself the nickname of '*Silver-tongued*

Parker' on account of his reputation as a 'wheeler-dealer'. In 1725 it seems he was 'caught out' because he was impeached on charges of corruption and malpractice and brought to trial before the House of Lords. He was removed from office and fined £30,000 - an absolute fortune at the time - although he retained his titles of Earl of Macclesfield and the Lord of the Manor of Leek.

The old Leek Grammar School of Lord Parker seen today

THE FRENCH CONNECTION

One interesting interlude in Leek's history was during the Napoleonic Wars when it was a parole town for French prisoners. Over 340 visitors passed through the town between 1803 and 1814, and they were billeted in houses around the town, mainly in the area of St Edward's church, Mill Street, Clerk Bank, St Edward Street and Derby Street.

Being on parole they were allowed a certain freedom to fraternise with the local townsfolk, and a number of them eventually married local girls and settled in Leek - leaving names like Magnier and Mien to this day. They were subject to the discipline of the local Parole Agent and had to attend a daily muster, but they comprised mainly of military and naval officers, and it is clear that they enjoyed a good lifestyle - they even formed a Masonic lodge of their own. Some escaped, and most of the others returned home by the end of the conflict. A few died in Leek and their graves can be found today in the northern section of St Edward's along with a modern Anglo-French memorial to them.

LEEK MARKETS

Leek's market charter was granted in 1208 in the reign of King John and reflected the importance of Dieulacres abbey. It gave the town the right to hold a weekly market, a tradition that has continued to this day, always on Wednesday. The Market Place is still a fine square in the centre of the town with an old Market cross. Traditionally the cross was the place where country women sold their butter, eggs and cheese. In 1897 the splendid Butter Market was built to house the booming trade in market produce and it is still in use today.

Gradually over the years the nature of the market changed away from local products but was still a great attraction. It now also has a busy Saturday antique and bric-a-brac market, and strangely enough the world has recently gone full circle and we are seeing once again 'farmers' markets' there.

From medieval times Leek has also had a livestock market. Animals were originally sold openly on the streets, for example the sheep market was alongside the Market Place, between the present Sheep Market and St Edward's Church. The Cattle Market covered much of the area that is now around the Monument.

Cattle, pigs, sheep and horses often wandered loose, and the occasional rampaging bull, and the work of cleaning up after the market was a messy business. By the middle of the 19th century there were so many complaints that in 1859 a purpose-built Smithfield market was constructed on land that is now the bus station and shopping centre. It had proper pens and accommodation for auctioneers, and it soon saw the development of many businesses to serve the large farming fraternity that made their weekly trip to market.

The market remained a much-loved feature of the town until the late 1960s when the local council decided that retail development was desirable in the town and the livestock market could be better served by new premises on town owned land at Barnfields. The loss of the traditional and 'famous' market, and the building of an architecturally poor 1960's retail block, have for long been regretted by many Leek folk and seen as a nail in the coffin of the town. But in another turn of the circle we now see the real prospect of the extension of the Steam Railway and the Caldon Canal into a site close to the modern livestock market, with great potential for tourism again.

Magnier, a French prisoner of war, stayed on in Leek and the family is still in the area today

Leek Market Place area in 1977.

Mention is made in many parts of this book of the activity of dame schools.
Marsland School seen here in Leek in Weston Road in the early 1900s was such.

Leek market at the beginning of the 20th century.

LEEK BUILDING SOCIETIES

Leek can claim a little fame for many things, from its old markets and silk industry, James Brindley, Sugden architecture, its Bayeux Tapestry, its William Morris connections, Adams Butter, its antique trade, right up to the modern success of businesses like Balls adhesives, IAE ('That Pole from Leek') and Cottage Delight foods. But perhaps above all of these it is its part in shaping the British Building Society movement that stands out.

The early headquarters of the Leek & Moorlands Building Society in Stockwell Street - now the Leek Council offices.

Today Leek has two mutual societies, one, Leek United, a solid local business, the other, Britannia, one of the largest in the country. Thrift and an eye to the future saw the development in thriving Victorian towns like Leek of various friendly societies and savings banks. The Leek & Moorlands Building Society was started in 1856 in Stockwell Street. It grew rapidly and in the 20th century metamorphosed through various mergers to the Leek & Westbourne B.S., the Leek & Eastern Counties B.S., and finally the Britannia.

The Leek United Permanent Benefit Building Society, later Leek United & Midland B.S., nowadays the Leek United, had as its Secretary in 1895 a man destined to become one of the most distinguished figures in the movement. Enoch Hill was born in Leek and worked first as a printer. From the Leek United he went in 1902 to the Halifax Permanent B.S. Between the wars, as Secretary, he took it from strength to strength, becoming the foremost society in the land. He was knighted in 1928.

SUGDEN & SONS, ARCHITECTS OF VICTORIAN LEEK

William Sugden, architect, was born in Keighley and came to Leek in his late 20s in 1849. His son William Larner Sugden was born here in 1850.

Sugden's prospered along with the silk trade in the late Victorian golden age of Leek and Sugden & Son were responsible for many of Leek's notable public buildings, including the Nicholson Institute, the Cottage Hospital, the Old Police Station, the NatWest Bank and the Congregational Church (Trinity). When the visitor to Leek walks the length of Derby Street and looks up at the fascinating Victorian architecture, many of these are 'Sugden' creations.

The Cottage Hospital and the Nicholson Institute seen here are both Sugden buildings. Both have been extensively refurbished in recent years to retain their special character for Leek.

Big Mill in Mill Street is an impressive Sugden-designed mill with an Italianate tower.

WALL GRANGE

This tiny hamlet stands on the banks of the River Churnet and was part of the settlement of Wall. The road between Leek and Longsdon crossed the Churnet at Wall, over a bridge that is thought to have been there in 1244. In the early 13th century, the Earls of Chester gave an estate at Wall to Trentham priory.

The Trentham priory estate at Wall included arable land and meadows and disputes with Dieulacres occurred from time to time, when the abbey claimed tithe payments. Settlement was reached when Trentham was granted exemption from paying tithes on land newly brought into cultivation.

Suggestions of a manor court at Wall in 1293 are unsubstantiated. A grange was established in the 13th century, well before the name Wall Grange begins to appear in the records in 1439. The house at Wall Grange was assessed for Hearth Tax in 1666, on eleven hearths. The house was rebuilt in 1715 by John Debank, of the family that married into the Sneyds.

After the dissolution, the estate was granted to Charles, Duke of Sutherland and Wall Grange descended through the Leveson, later the Leveson-Gower, family until 1911 when it was sold to its tenant, Robert Bennison.

We can record the following Leveson-Gower tenants:

1484	Hugh Egerton
1509-1510	William Egerton
1537	Lawrence Savage. A relative of the Egertons
1558	Sir Ralph Egerton and William Egerton
1571	Timothy Egerton. Died without issue
1584	Edward Tyrrel. Second husband of Timothys' wife
1606	Thomas Egerton of Adstock, Bucks
1620	Timothy Egerton. Son of Thomas of Adstock
1628	Thomas Egerton
1640s	Thomas Egerton. Cousin
1649	Mrs Egerton. Widow

The estate was sequestered in 1654 and held by parliamentarian, Col. Edward Downes.

1654	Death of Colonel Downes
1668	Lease acquired by William Jolliffe of Leek
1669	Thomas Jolliffe
1694	Simon Debank
	Mary Debank Widow
	John Debank. Son
	Simon Debank. Younger son
1758	Thomas Royle
1790	Vernon Royle
Gap occurs	
1825	Henry West
1859-1891	Son of Henry West

Wallgrange brickworks.

The canal feeder close to
Wallgrange.

The Caldon Canal at Horse
Bridge, moored at what was
Wallgrange brickworks.

During the industrial revolution the Caldon canal and the Stoke to Leek railway arrived. Bricks had been made locally for many years, with brickmaking kilns recorded at Ladderedge and Longsdon but by 1881 the major brickmaking enterprise was at Horse Bridge, Wall Grange,

Deep Haye reservoir and Wallgrange station, where passengers for St Edward's Hospital alighted.

adjacent to both canal and railway. The Wall Grange brickworks provided bricks for the new St Edwards Hospital in 1892 when access was along Wall Lane, the route of the original greenway to Wall Grange, Longsdon and Denford.

St Edward's Hospital - originally the County Lunatic Asylum - was built on the high land of Wall above the Churnet. It housed around 1200 patients at its peak in the 1930s. The hospital closed in the 1990s and has since been developed as houses and the Leek Rugby Club. The main entrance building and water tower are the only buildings that survive.

Rudyard Lake in the days of steam and below, seen from the south end today.

LEEKBROOK

Leekbrook was little more than the confluence of the brook and the Churnet. The original Joshua Wardle factory, the 'old works', has long since been replaced by modern industrial units and now the 'new works' has been demolished to be replaced by houses. The only link with the endeavours of the Wardles is the Travellers Rest which originally stood by the works and was rebuilt on its present site when they built their new factory.

RUDYARD LAKE

Rudyard Lake is a reservoir for the Caldon Canal, supplying it through a feeder that follows the course of the Churnet into Leek. The construction of the lake was authorised by an Act of Parliament of 1797. By Victorian times and the coming of the railway along its edges, the lake became a pleasure resort for thousands. The station, opening in 1849, was on the Churnet Valley Line of the North Staffordshire Railway ('The Knotty') which ran from North Rode through Leek and on to Rocester and Uttoxeter.

Regattas were held on the lake in Victorian times and by the Edwardian era the boating, pleasure fair, skating rink, cafes and hotels made it a favourite holiday for the industrial populations of the area. It remained a great venue for cyclists right into the second half of the 20th century. Today it is mainly a walking venue although it has a sailing club and many fishermen. And famously, during the years that John Lockwood Kipling was at the Burslem School of Art he courted his wife-to-be there and when their first child was born they named him Rudyard in fond recollection.

THE WARDLES

Originally from Ipstones, Joshua Wardle found employment as a stone mason in Sutton near Macclesfield, a trade which Joseph his son would also follow. When Joseph married he named a son Joshua after his grandfather. Joshua grew up as a Macclesfield boy and when he was old enough to start work, he joined Park Green dye works instead of following the family tradition of masons.

He quickly established himself as capable pupil. He noticed that a large amount of the silks dyed by the factory came from Leek and this stood him in good stead when at the age of twenty-seven he started his own business. Leek was the obvious place to him - premises were freely available and the Churnet had long been known for the soft water so essential for the dyeing of silks.

The flat meadow land where the Leek Brook joined the Churnet was ideal for Joshua's dream and he immediately set about raising the capital to purchase the land and build his factory. By 1830 Joshua was pouring all his energy into his new business, and he had a house built for his young wife and family just across the road from the new factory.

Thomas, the first of their six children attended the village school at Cheddleton for a while but Joshua considered the school too small for his son and he became a boarder at a school in Macclesfield for several years. Towards the end of his education he returned to the family home and attended the grammar school in Leek.

Joshua made sure that his son learned every aspect of the silk dyeing industry and he instilled into Thomas his own desire to master the art of dyeing - in Joshua's case his great success was with Raven Black. For Thomas the great challenge would become the dyeing of Tussur silk. This natural silk is the product of a silk moth in abundance in the forests of India but the problem was that Tussur unlike Chinese silk was almost impossible to dye. For the next decade, Thomas wrestled with the problem, even visiting Kashmir to pursue it.

Whilst Joshua had been the astute entrepreneur, Thomas had the superior education and an analytical mind. By microscopic examination Thomas noticed that the silk fibres were joined by a resinous glue called sericin. He found a way to remove the glue, enabling the fibres to absorb the dyes. The work was to take many years. Different dyes were introduced, first greys, then various primary colours and finally strong yellows, a pale blue, a red and a mixtures of hues. By 1872 his work was complete. His knowledge of the dyeing process was the greatest in the land and would pay rich dividends in the years that followed.

Thomas also noted that a large amount of waste was created that could not be used for weaving. Dyeing some of it black, he invited local firms to produce a short pile fabric. The lack of enthusiasm led Thomas to take the waste to Crefeld in Germany where a material was produced that was rich, soft and glossy, and Thomas returned home in triumph. Thomas, along with his brother, George, decided to exhibit both the Tussur silks and the new material which they called Sealcloth. The exhibition was a great success and the Leekbrook works went from strength to strength. His achievements were recognised in 1875 when he was elected a Fellow of the Chemical Society.

The dye works of Samuel Tatton at Hencroft in Leek was acquired about this time for the sum of £3,550 and included in the sale was a building across the road that Thomas named the Churnet Works. Among the first people to use the facilities at Hencroft was William Morris. Morris & Co. had worked on several windows in Cheddleton church during the restoration work carried out by Sir Gilbert Scott. William Morris, poet, designer and socialist, was a meticulous man who demanded perfection in everything. For a period of six years, from 1875 to 1881, he and Thomas developed a close professional relationship, the net result of which was the wonderful, natural designs and colours that set Morris apart from the rest.

Thomas, who by now had moved into his house in Spout Street in Leek, remained a close friend until Morris died in 1896. Thomas's brother in law, George Wardle, worked closely with Morris and eventually joined Morris & Co, in time became responsible for the day to day running of the company.

The greatest recognition of the Wardle family came in 1897. The Queen's new year honours' list announced that Thomas had been given a knighthood for services to the silk industry. He was recognised as one of the great figures of the silk weaving and dyeing industry. Sir Thomas and Lady Wardle had a little over a decade to enjoy their fame - Thomas died in January 1909.

Although the silk industry continued to prosper for several more decades, the seeds of change had been sewn in the mid-1840s with the duty on imported silks removed and the growth of free trade. The advances made by the likes of Joshua and Thomas Wardle still enabled the trade to enjoy full employment for many years to come but changes were inevitable. The accelerated use of man-made fibres after the 1939-1945 war and international competition meant the dependency of Leek on the silk and dyeing industry would slowly end. In the 1960s Leek was still predominantly a mill town, mills small and large jostling cheek by jowl with the streets of terraced houses. But now in the 21st century the textile mills are all but gone, many replaced by housing, the architecturally valuable preserved as flats, residential homes and antique businesses.

THE BAYEUX TAPESTRY AND MRS ELIZABETH WARDLE

The original Bayeux Tapestry is preserved in Bayeux in Normandy and was commissioned by Bishop Odo in about 1070. Odo was the half brother of William the Conquerer and he was ideally placed to ensure a French bias.

Whether it is the work of William's wife, Matilda, and the ladies of her court, or English embroiderers from Kent, is debated, although it now appears that the stitchcraft points towards English hands. It is in fact an embroidery, measuring 230ft in length and 20 inches wide.

The making of a full size replica is almost entirely due to the enterprise of Elizabeth Wardle, the wife of Thomas Wardle. Elizabeth bore Thomas fourteen children, nine of whom survived into adulthood. Despite this she developed her own interests, and foremost among these was the art of embroidery.

Thomas and Elizabeth were friends of Sir Philip Cunliffe-Owen, director of the South Kensington Museum (later the Victoria and Albert). On a visit to London in 1885, Sir Philip showed them a number of cartoons of the famous Bayeux Tapestry commissioned in 1871. They made an immediate impression

Sir Thomas Wardle and his wife Lady Wardle, pictured
here, brought fame and fortune to the town.
Sir Thomas was involved in Leek with William Morris in
developing the dyes for his fabric designs. It has much
to do with the pre-Raphaelite connections in Leek and
Cheddleton churches. He was knighted for his work in
advancing the dyeing of silks.
Lady Wardle established and developed the Leek
Embroidery Society which was nationally recognised,
and famously produced the replica of the Bayeux tapestry
housed in Reading today.
Middle - a section of the tapestry
Below - Three Marys altar cloth produced for Cheddleton
church now in the Nicholson Institute.

on Elizabeth, fascinated by the use of embroidery on such a large scale. She determined that England should have its own facsimile of the Tapestry and that her friends and colleagues in Leek should be involved in its creation.

A visit to Bayeux followed and, in typical Wardle fashion, a close examination of the original work was undertaken. On their return, Thomas selected 100 pounds of the finest worsted wools, which he dyed with vegetable dyes to match the eight original colours. Elizabeth, the founder of the Leek Embroidery Society, had little trouble in persuading local needlewomen to join her in this exciting task. There were thirty-five members of the Society mostly from the town itself, including Elizabeth and two of her daughters.

Elizabeth borrowed the cartoons and from these Miss Lizzie Allen traced the details precisely onto the linen base. The embroidery was applied to panels onto which the needlewomen added their signatures beneath the portion they had completed. Elizabeth stitched a final section which reads. *'This production of the Bayeux Tapestry was worked in Leek in Staffordshire. The drawings were lent by the Authorities of the South Kensington Museum. 35 ladies have been engaged on this piece of tapestry and the names of each will be found underneath her work. E. Wardle. Whitsuntide 1886. The worsteds were dyed in permanent colours by Thomas Wardle, F.C.S. FGS.'*

Mrs Clara Bill stitched together the completed panels. Clara was of German extraction and had married into the Bill family of Farley and in later years she helped to run the Leek Embroidery Society

The final resting place of the facsimile is a story in itself and does little credit to the people of Leek. It was exhibited in Leek in 1886 in the Nicholson Institute, where it was seen by 1,207 people. Before the end of the year, it was exhibited in Tewkesbury, Newcastle-upon-Tyne, Stoke-on-Trent, Worcester, Chester, America and Germany. The Society formed a company in the hope that money raised by the exhibitions would support the venture. In 1892, the tapestry was seen at Brighton, Blackpool, Nottingham and Derby, and in 1893 it was awarded a Gold Medal in the National Workmens Exhibition. Despite all this success, Leek did not see fit to offer it a home.

In 1895, the tapestry was displayed in Reading Town Hall and Alderman Arthur Hill offered the sum of £300 for its purchase. The Society 'company' took a vote amongst its members and the offer was accepted. Elizabeth was devastated: *'I never thought we should allow such a treasured possession to be sold and leave Leek'*. Leek's loss was Reading's gain. Even Queen Victoria took an interest in the tapestry and Arthur Hill was commanded to take it to Windsor for a viewing. Today the tapestry is on permanent display in specially designed, illuminated cases that allow its full length to be viewed at leisure.

There are many interesting old
buildings in Leek. Right we see
the old parish church of St
Edwards and Clerk Bank with
Naylor's Yard beyond.

St Edward street is full of
all sorts of architecture.
Many of the buildings were
originally residences of the
more wealthy of Leek.

THE NICHOLSONS

The Nicholsons originated from Yorkshire. Joshua, 1812-1885, served his apprenticeship in Bradford and came to Leek at the age of twenty-five to take up a position of representative with the firm of J & J Brough & Co. He quickly made his mark in the town - he was a Congregationalist, a Liberal and a Free Trader and in his first year in Leek he helped to found the Mechanics Institute.

He helped to expand the business to such an extent that in the course of time he became a partner in the firm, and when Joshua and John Brough retired in 1868, he became principal partner in a large and progressive mill.

The family lived in some style, first at Greystones and later at Stockwell House and Joshua's two sons, Joshua Oldfield and Arthur were foremost amongst the local gentry. It is to Joshua that the town owes the Nicholson Institute, which he intended has an opportunity for the youth of the town for study and learning and a memorial to Richard Cobden, the reformer.

The Institute has long served the town as library, arts centre and educational establishment. It was built by H & R Inskip & Son, of Longton to the design of Sugden & Son for £20,000. It was opened by the Lord Lieutenant of Staffordshire, Lord Wrottesley in 1884.

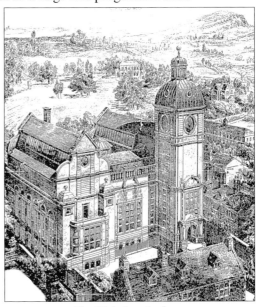

The Nicholson Institute

Joshua died in 1885 and it was left to his sons to follow the standards established by their father. A hard act to follow but Joshua Oldfield Nicholson and Sir Arthur Nicholson did their father proud. Arthur was educated at Leek and Huddersfield after which he joined the firm as an apprentice. By 1868 he was a partner and eventually he became head of the firm for 30 years.

Arthur did much to establish the company among the leaders of the silk industry. In 1882, he married Marianne Falkner of Frodsham and three sons and a daughter followed. In 1885 he purchased the Highfield estate.

Arthur was active in all areas of society. In 1889 he became Leek's first County Councillor, elected unopposed. He was a member of the County Education Committee, and Chairman of the Governors at Westwood Girls High

School. He was involved in the Leek & Moorlands Building Society and true to his Liberal upbringing, was President of the Leek Liberal Association. In 1911 he was knighted in Asquith's government, for services to the silk industry and for his contributions to the Liberal Party.

The war of 1914-1918 brought particular sadness to the town as many local men lost their lives and among those was Basil Nicholson, Arthur's youngest son. To honour the dead of Leek and their son, the Nicholson's gave the War Memorial clock tower to the town as a permanent reminder of the price paid in pursuit of democracy. Leek's 'Monument', built of fine portland stone, still stands today as a fine landmark in the centre of Leek.

In 1913, Sir Arthur and Lady Nicholson entertained George V and Queen Mary at Highfield, on the occasion of the Royal visit to Leek. The King and Sir Arthur shared a common interest, both enthusiastic breeders of shire horses and the Highfield Stud provided a display of shires for the King's inspection.

Sir Arthur seen with George V

Sir Arthur died in 1929 and, fittingly, his body was conveyed in a plain oak coffin to the Congregational Church on a farm dray, drawn by his two favourite horses, Leek Queen and Leek Pearl.

ADAMS BUTTER - SPREADING EVERYWHERE

Among the businesses on the Barnfields estate is Kerrygold, the Irish dairy producer. Its presence in Leek is related to the story of Adams Butter.

The Adams family occupied a dairy farm that straddled the Buxton road in the early 1870s. The farm, and later the factory, lay on the corner of Buxton and Springfield roads. The fields that lay on either side of the road have long since

Adams: The old farm in Buxton Road and two early vehicles.

succumbed to suburbia, and houses, a supermarket and light industry have now replaced what was Adams Butter 30 years ago.

Fifty years on from the 1870s, a young Fred Adams, as well as delivering milk to his customers, was also delivering his farm-made butter. The demand for Fred's butter exceeded all expectations and the farm was soon unable to produce enough. Fred, very much the entrepreneur, overcame the problem by buying butter from other farms in the area and repacking it under his own label.

Demand for Fred's butter spread to local towns and villages at an amazing rate, and was even more in demand when his tiny workforce began to cut and wrap butter in convenient ¹/2lb packs. The answer was to build a factory, or more precisely, to convert one of the farm buildings, and Adams Butter was born. As the business progressed, so did Fred's entrepreneurial spirit. A steam lorry, unique in those days, appeared on the scene and a few years later a fleet of vans conveyed merchandisers across the length and breadth of the country.

But still demand outstripped supply. To manage the rapidly growing company, Fred's family joined him. Butter was imported from Ireland, then Scandinavia. and the family farm, for so long the hub of the business, was replaced by a purpose built factory. Modern machinery was introduced. and a fleet of lorries delivered pre-packed, blended butter to all parts of the British Isles. The same lorries called at the docks to collect bulk butter.

The fleet of lorries grew to 200, including refrigerated vehicles developed by Adams engineers and forerunners of today's temperature controlled vehicles. By the 1960s, butter was being shipped to Leek from all over the world, including Australia and New Zealand. Adams became the pioneers of the mini pack for the airlines, and plastic tubs of butter for the catering industry. At its peak in the 1970s, Adams had an annual production rate of 57,200 tons per annum. In terms of ¹/2lb packs, 57,200 tons equates to 256,256,000 units. Such tremendous volume turned Adams Butter, *'SPREADING EVERYWHERE'*, into the largest supplier in the world, with sales in excess of £80 million per annum.

If Fred Adams started his business at just the right time, the family knew just when to sell. Supermarkets were starting to make their presence felt in the 1970s and in 1971, the Irish Dairy Board purchased 25% of the shares. The following year a further purchase gave the Irish Dairy Board 51% and the remaining shares were purchased in 1976.

For a while, the Adams name lived on but they decided to concentrate on the rapidly growing cheese market, Kerrygold closed its Buxton road factory and moved to a new site on the Barnfields Industrial Estate. By the 1990s, Adams Foods was confined to the history books and the archives of an ex-employee, Alan Smith, whose knowledge is the basis of this précis.

Chapter Three
Cheddleton

OLD CHEDDLETON & ITS MILLS

The road from Longsdon to Wall Grange passes close to Deep Haye, a small reservoir developed by the Potteries Water board during the mid-1800s to supply clean water to Stoke-on-Trent following a typhoid epidemic. The water feeding the reservoir drains the higher points of Cheddleton parish around Crown Point, Brund and Shaffalong, spring water of 'exceptional' quality.

The road, Park Lane, derived its name from Cheddleton Park. Although parkland is found elsewhere in Cheddleton there can be little doubt that this park belonged to the Lords of the Manor, the de Chetletons. Park Lane eventually merges with Shaffalong lane a few hundred yards away from the church, but before that point a track which may have been the original road turns to the left and passes behind the church before merging with the road leading to Hall House. By common consent, Hall House occupies the site of the original manor house. It is from here, around the Hall and the Church that the village of Cheddleton evolved. From its vantage point high above the Churnet, the de Chetletons were Lords of all they surveyed.

From the plateau occupied by Hall House the land falls away abruptly on three sides, granting easy access only from the west. To the north the land falls, in the space of a hundred yards, to the level of the river where the water mills still stand. Here the canal towpath follows the easy walk to Longsdon, Denford and the Horse Bridge on the fringe of Wall Grange.

The water mills are still in working order through the endeavours of Industrial Heritage Trust. Surprisingly, the Domesday book does not mention a mill in its entry for Cheddleton:

'The Earl holds Celtetone himself, and William from him. Half a hide, Land for four ploughs. In Lordship half a plough, woodland half a league long and three furlongs wide. (In modern parlance 60 acres of plough-lands, 32 oxen and 4 ploughs) *The Lord of the Manor has four oxen and, four villagers each hold a small amount of land with four oxen between them. There is also one hundred and eighty acres of woodlands.'*

As there is no mention of a mill in Basford, Consall or Rownall either, you are left wondering where the corn was ground. One explanation may lie with the devastation that followed the conquest. Many of the local Saxon overlords resisted strongly before being finally subjugated by William. Large tracts of land and villages were laid to waste in the struggle. Could a mill have existed prior to the conquest, only to have been destroyed by the Normans?

Robert Copeland was instrumental in saving the mills from dereliction and he quotes an Inquisition during the reign of Henry III in 1253, when it was recorded that *'the mill at Chetelton was in the possession of Roger'*. The mill is mentioned again in 1580 when a reference is made to *'two mills under one roof, one for fulling and one for corn'*. Among the subsequent owners of the mills are the Finney family, Henry Biggins and Thomas Hammersley.

Robert Copeland's ancestor, Ralph Wood, was the owner of the mills in 1720. Ralph has the distinction of being known as the `honest miller', as inscribed on the life size bust of his grandson, Enoch Wood, the famous potter: `*My grandfather, Ralph Wood, died aged 77 buried at Cheddleton, March 1753, he was a honest miller, and ground all the oatmeal in the neighbourhood at his three mills at Burslem, Cheddleton and Bells mill at Shelton, he worked two days at each mill.'*

Ralph's sons, Ralph and Aaron became prominent potters.

The original mill, now referred to as the south mill, started life with a single wheel, although a second wheel was added early on. Corn grinding and fulling were the essential ingredients of the trade. Fulling relates to the wool trade. The breeding of sheep was common throughout the monastic period and fulling was a process that enhanced the quality and thickness of the wool prior to weaving. Virtually all the mills on the Churnet, including those under the control of Rocester and Dieulacres abbeys, were aligned to the wool trade.

Versatility was the name of the game and Cheddleton played it well. So well in fact, that a second mill was built in the 19th century, to contend with the volume of business that followed the opening of the Caldon canal. The canal system opened up the nation to trade previously limited by the horse and cart. Suddenly transportation of goods became smoother, quicker and wider. Breakages and costs were reduced and the packhorse became an expensive and archaic option.

Among the first to benefit were the pottery industries in Stoke-on-Trent. The water mills began to grind flint for the potters as well as accommodating the demands of trades proliferating in the Churnet Valley. Ironstone and limestone found its way to the Cheddleton mills. The latter was also smelted in two small kilns near to the mills as well in the much larger kilns behind the canal wharf a few hundred yards away. It is also thought that ochre was produced in small quantities. Ochre is a pigment made of fine clay and iron oxide. Both products were in abundance in the Churnet Valley and the pottery

Cheddleton c.1960 showing Harry Bold's shop on the right and the old Tanyard, the 3-storey building in the background. Wall Lane Terrace is on the skyline with Higger's hill in front.

The flint mills at Cheddleton.

Churnet Hall 2004.

Cheddleton Station in pre-Beeching days.

industry had a growing need for dyes and pigments.

If the canals were responsible for the water mills reaching their peak, the railways and steam power were responsible for their decline. The industrial revolution and improved transportation brought to an end almost a thousand years of milling in this delightful little spot overlooked by the Hall and the Church. Will any of our modern industries last so long?

The large, plain building standing close to the canal towpath, is Churnet Hall. The bottom part of the building is built from local stone and gives every indication of once being a single storey. Two more storeys in a red brick have been added and do little for the eye, although the bricks may well be of local origin, and the tall square chimney indicates the building's industrial heritage. The alterations appear to have been made to accommodate a silk mill that occupied the site from 1838 until about 1855. The 180 dozen spindles, used for throwing silk, and the seven looms, were worked by a 6 HP steam engine.

In the basements of the nearby houses, the local Cheddleton bitter was brewed and no doubt the Churnet Hall was used to store the hops, bottles and barrels. The village supported many pubs, although the local brewery did not have all its own way. Brewers from Leek, Wetley Rocks and Burslem competed to quench the thirst of the regulars at the Bridge Inn, Red Lion, Black Lion, Boat, Fox, Bell and Railway Hotel.

The Bridge Inn, the Red Lion and the Boat Inn prospered with the opening of the Caldon canal. By the same token, trade suffered when the canal was superseded by the railway. The Bridge Inn closed its doors when the boat building and wharf trade diminished. In doing so it brought about fresh opportunities. The Bridge Inn became the village store and for the best part of a hundred years the Bold family supplied the village with its everyday needs.

The store is now just a lovely memory for those born before the days of supermarkets. The smell of beeswax, the polished wooden floor, the brass scales to weigh tea and sugar, the sacks of flour and bags of sultanas. On the wooden shelves stood round cheeses wrapped in cheese cloth, ready to be cut and wrapped, in an age that would not have recognised plastic shrink wrap. The cheeses breathed and matured and were better for it. The bacon, without the benefit of additives, was cut from the side of a well-salted pig. It had to end of course. The village shop cannot compete with the supermarket - and today it is the village restaurant that provides the aromas.

The popularity of Bold's shop coincided with a new popularity of the Churnet Hall. The silk trade may account for the second storey and in more recent years a label printing business thrived on that floor, but in the 1950s and 1960s the mood was lighter as the austerity of war receded. Film shows and whist drives were held but most popular by far was the village dance each Saturday night - Old Time, of course. The band, more corn miller than Glen Miller, was accompanied by a crooner who had cultivated his thin moustache for style. As the band belted out the music, the young bloods displayed the fancy footwork vital for the Lancers and the Gay Gordons. During the interval the Red Lion provided the Dutch courage, the moonlight and canal provided the romance, and the young village girls demonstrated the art of diminishing return.

As for drugs and violence, this was an age of innocence. Such things belonged to American films or London gangsters. Altercations did occur from time to time but were usually limited to a great deal of posturing and threats that fizzled out to nothing.

THE VILLAGE DANCE

On a warm summer night when our fancy took flight
And the music was lively and gay.
As Johnny Pitt sang, his song with the Band,
We danced in the old fashioned way.

When the girl in your dreams, is elusive, it seems
And you are all too aware of your faults.
You still take a chance, and you ask her to dance.
And she smiles and says yes to the waltz

And she, so polite, so gracious and light,
takes your hand as you walk to the floor.
And you dance and you twirl with the sweet village girl
And, you can't ask for anything more.

And later that night, when you leave the bright lights,
you are pleased to have taken the chance.
And you dream of the Miss and the quick stolen kiss,
on the night that you went to the dance.

Alan Gibson

Across the road from the Churnet Hall, Castro's now occupies the site of Bold's shop and the lime kilns just below have long since had their openings blocked.The stone building opposite was once the workshop of the boat repairer.

The cottages at the beginning of Station road were once the Railway Hotel which slaked the thirst of the workers from the nearby skinyard. The purist would call it a 'tannery' where in the two-storey terraced houses, now sadly demolished, workers toiled in the basement and the stench permeated throughout. 'Skinyard' is far more realistic. The job was taken on by the desperate and a fancy title did little to make you smell any better. Tradition has it that Isaac Findler, a local artist of some repute, lived here. Robert Milner, local historian, believes that Isaac would have lived at the Adam's Flint and Colour mill, where his father was employed.

The tannery, the canal wharf, the boat repairers and the brewery are long gone. The last of the brewers are still around, or at least their family name. Mrs Kent and her sons John, James and Reuben ran the brewery in the 1890s until it closed in 1915. Kelly's Directory of 1892 gives Mary Kent as landlady of the Red Lion and in 1896 William Burton is given as managing partner of the Cheddleton Brewery Co. The Kents are still in the village, although the Smiths from 1859 and John Illsey have faded from local memory. Illsey, as well as being the local brewer, owned the Travellers Rest at Leekbrook. He was related to the Wardle family.

THE SNEYDS

From ancient times the Sneyds were major landowners in North Staffordshire and the 'Keele' Sneyds, like others at the time, gained great wealth through land enclosure and industrial development, eg coal mining. The 'Churnet' Sneyds were a poorer branch of the family, often appearing to live beyond their means, but they were the Lords of the Manor and amongst the first order of Gentry in the area in the early 19th century. In the mid 19th century they owned considerable property and land in the area,

To put the matter into some perspective, I will relate two asides that have remained with me since childhood. One involves a conversation between my father and David Scott Moncrieff that took place at Ashcombe Park Cricket Club. David stretched his arm across the horizon and said *'from here, the Sneyd's owned all the land as far as the eye can see'*. That seemed a lot to me at the time. I was to learn later that it was but a small part of the Sneyd's land.

David's wife, Averil Scott Moncrieff [née Sneyd] of Basford Hall is responsible for the other aside. Years ago, she gave me a letter of introduction to the librarian at Keele University, a former home of the Sneyds. *'You may find it difficult,'* she said *'to trace our family history, but we are reasonably certain that we go back to Alfred the Great'.*

I will simply list all the properties that fall within the Churnet Valley area that were occupied by the Sneyds in the 19th century: Ashcombe Park was built by James Trubshaw in 1807 for the Rev. John Sneyd. The site was previously occupied by Botham Hall quakers who had long since moved to Apesford near Basford. In later years, other notable families lived at Ashcombe including the

Ashcombe

Basford

Sharpcliffe

Wardles, of silk dyeing fame and the Haighs, directors of Brittain's Paper Mills.

Basford Hall was once part of the Loxley estate, Uttoxeter. The Kinnersleys of Loxley Hall married into the Sneyds and by 1810, Basford was occupied by the Sneyds. It has remained a Sneyd home ever since and is currently occupied by Humphrey and Judy Scott Moncrieff.

Barrow Hill, Rocester, was a late 18th century house remodelled by Trubshaw for a Mr Birch. Later, it was the home of William and Jane Sneyd before passing to Mr M.A.White and then to Captain Henry Dawson. The house was latterly owned by the Bamfords before becoming a Nursing Home.

Belmont Hall was built around 1770 for the Rev. John Sneyd. When the Sneyds moved from Belmont it was owned by a succession of tenants, some of whom were businessmen involved with the mining operations in the Churnet Valley, and who appear later in our story.

Moss Lee Farm, near to Ipstones was a part of the Belmont estate.

Sharpecliffe Hall, near Ipstones is an 11th century manor house purchased by Rev. John Sneyd for his son in law, Ralph Debank.

Woodlands Hall, Cheddleton, among the smallest of the Sneyd houses, stands on an eminence overlooking the Caldon canal and the Churnet Valley. It was built in 1832 for Thomas Sneyd but initially occupied by Rev. Henry Sneyd.

BRITTAIN'S PAPER MILLS

For a long time, a huge paper making complex occupied the land on the banks of the Churnet for a mile between the Leek road and Basford Bridge Lane. The land is now occupied by a multitude of industrial units. At the western end, the more modern of the old paper mills survive as part of the factory of Batemans, manufacturers of agricultural metalwork. Nearby is AP Chemicals and at the eastern end a modern factory houses the adhesive manufacturer, F.H. Ball.

The closure of Brittain's Paper Mills was a huge loss to the village because for almost two hundred years the paper mills had found employment for the people of Cheddleton. Despite humble beginnings the workforce grew from the first few on Butchers Meadows to over a thousand people with production twenty-four hours a day.

The Butchers Meadows site was in use long before William Adams purchased the land from the Rev. Powys in 1797. The Adams collection states *'the mill is situated on the banks of the Churnet - used as a flint and colour mill and now converted and applied to the manufacture of paper.'* The Churnet was again being used as waste disposal for the dyeing industry.

William Adams was among the foremost pottery manufacturers of the time. His need was for a specialist paper for the transfer of decorative designs

Brittain's Paper Mills 1920s

The Churnet in flood at Brittain's - the river has flooded in many parts over the centuries,
but it is nowadays far less likely to flood because of changes along its course.

and the Adams family would use the Cheddleton paper-making factory for several decades. In 1838, Sarah Sophia Adams and Ann Adams leased to Thomas Day, James Mobey and William Ash *'all the water, flint and colour mill on the banks of the Churnet at Cheddleton with a convenient way into the mill for the manufacture of paper'.* The lease also included a new water wheel. Later that year Thomas Day and Thomas Appleby as tenants.

The Adams family retained ownership until 1854 when Ann, who had inherited Sophia's share, sold the mill to George Hulme, thus ending the Adam's association with the Cheddleton mill.

Running parallel to the success of the Cheddleton mill was the Ivy House mill at Hanley which had installed a Fourdrinier paper-making machine in 1827. They competed strongly with the Adams mill and at one stage virtually put them out of business. Action was called for and the Cheddleton mill was leased to Edward Newman Fourdrinier who promptly modernised the factory and replaced the hand-made paper by installing a Fourdrinier machine. He remained at Cheddleton from 1844 to 1849 when the mill was offered for sale and purchased by Goldstraw and Hulme.

In 1855, George Hulme, Charles Hough and William Goldstraw were granted a patent *'for the improvement of machinery or apparatus for the manufacture of paper'.* By 1862 William Goldstraw had become the dominant force and he purchased the mill prior to selling it to his son Samuel who would live and work at the paper mill until his death in 1888. The mill was then left in trust to his wife. Among Samuel's executives was one Jeremiah Steele, his son-in-law, who became the manager of the mill.

At the Hanley factory another familiar name emerged. In 1855, Thomas Brittain, a local banker, took over the business from the Fourdriniers. He was joined by his son, also Thomas, and in 1870 a third partner, Frederick Haigh. Haigh was instrumental in Brittain's coming to Cheddleton when he formed a partnership with Jeremiah Steele in 1889 and took over the Cheddleton mill.

In 1890, Ivy House and Cheddleton combined to form Brittain's Ltd. More machines were added and production increased dramatically. Ivy House specialised in pottery transfer papers and the Cheddleton mills in a wide range of technical grade tissues - bible paper, condenser paper and carbonised paper. Under the control of Frederick Haigh and, later his son, Alfred, Brittain's outgrew its humble origins, and land was purchased for expansion as the company competed for the global market. New mills were added every few years until fourteen paper mills were producing tissues on a grand scale.

With the vision of hindsight, the beginning of the end came in 1959 when Brittain's became a public company. Frederick and Alfred had died leaving

John Haigh to continue the family tradition. A public company, the issuing of shares and a shift of power brought inevitable change. For a while the company continued to prosper and a series of diversifications seemed appropriate - the dependence upon a single commodity did not rest easy with the new directors.

But Brittain's expanded into uncharted waters. Overdrafts and loans became the norm as expansion continued into engineering, transport, plastics, construction and plant hire. Chinese and Scandinavian paper manufacturers left Brittain's struggling to compete and the company, so long in the hands of the family, now began to look vulnerable. John Haigh, the last of the family, resigned as the company moved away from his ideals. In 1979 the financial institutions withdrew their support and the company went into receivership.

The gulf was visible for several years. Buildings decayed and a general air of neglect fell over this once thriving estate. Then, as the village came to terms with the job losses, other industries began to creep in. Chemicals and engineering began to replace paper as the main employer of labour. Slowly the area attracted other businesses and the Churnet Side Business Park developed.

F. H. BALL AND CO LTD

The Ball family hide their light under a bushel; for well over a century they have been quietly developing an important national business. Now, in the early years of a new millennium, the company is the Country's largest independent manufacturer of flooring adhesives and employ 120 people in modernised premises in a pleasant part of the old paper mill estate, where they moved in 1993.

The firm set out to make adhesives and inks for the shoe and harness trades in 1886, founded by Frances Ball in Lower Kennington Lane, south east London. Frances and his partner William Cowburn developed 'Ball's Invisible Patching Cement' for the patching of leather boots. From a small factory with a cobbled yard, they delivered their goods by hand in a two-wheeled barrow, or larger loads by horse and cart.

When Frances died in 1904, his son Walter took control. When Walter died, in 1931, ownership passed to his wife Lillie and their sons, Frank and Walter. In 1933 they moved to Tooting where the company's famous 'Stycco' brand of adhesives was produced in 1936 for use with webbing to join carpets.

The 1939-1945 war brought great changes for the family when they were listed as suppliers to the Ministry of Aircraft Production and asked to move away from the bombing of London. They moved to North Staffordshire and small premises in the village of Rudyard. After the war they acquired a one acre site on the edge of Leek and from here the company grew from a small local business to a national and innovative company.

The future for F.H. Ball can only be guessed at. They have adhesives for spun concrete pipes and for fibreglass on the decks of minesweepers. New adhesives are being tested in the searing heat of the deserts of the Middle East and on North Sea oil rigs with cushioned floor covering.

THE BEAUTIFUL CHURNET VALLEY
We leave the village where Basford Bridge lane reaches the bottom of the valley and crosses the old green road which led from Grange Farm towards Consall and Wetley Rocks, following the river and canal. The road was there long before the Navigation Inn (now the Boat Inn) was built and may even run close to the ancient boundary referred to as the Linus Britannicus.

The traveller would do well to pause a while at this busy junction. The railway station, the goodsyard, the pub and two ancient bridges compete for your attention. On the east side of the Churnet bridge channels have been cut between bends in the river in an attempt to ease the flooding that was a recurring problem for the paper mills. These days, picnics and fishing are the order of the day and the revived Churnet Valley Railway attracts visitors from far and wide for a trip down memory lane. Ongoing renovation has enabled the line to be re-opened between Leekbrook and Froghall and will, no doubt, eventually reach Oakamoor - and Leek.

As we journey towards Consall the landscape changes. The steep sides of the valley become densely wooded as native trees and flora clothe the hillsides. Stone edifices occur and man-made monuments bear witness to the Industrial Revolution. It is hard to imagine how busy this tranquil area used to be. Gone are the palls of smoke that hung above the trees, the drop hammers of the forge no longer reverberate along the valley, and water wheels no longer turn. Limestone and iron-ore no longer attract the entrepreneur and the demise of the charcoal burner leaves the trees to grow in peace. Hamlets that grew into busy industrial villages have now returned to 'grass roots'.

To appreciate the significance of the industrial revolution and the effects it had on the Churnet valley, we should now consider the canal and the railway, the limestone quarries and the extraction of iron ore. Even more important, we should consider the contribution of the Cheadle Brass Works and Thomas Bolton's at Oakamoor, looking also at the evidence that suggests the area was home to industrial man long before the industrial revolution

CALDON CANAL AND THE GRAND TRUNK CANAL
The need for navigable waterways throughout the country had been apparent for many years. As early as 1717, Thomas Congreave had proposed a navigable

waterway between the Severn and the Trent. The proposal fared little better than its predecessor - an act of parliament in 1699 was granted to improve navigation on the River Trent between Wilden Ferry in Derbyshire and Burton-on-Trent in Staffordshire.

In reality, both schemes were ahead of their time. The ideas were sound but the will was lacking. Fifty years later a different picture emerged. The cost of land transport was prohibitive and the carrying capacity limited - trade and expansion were confined.

The introduction of the Grand Trunk Canal scheme captured the imagination, and more importantly, the financial support, of business leaders who saw greater trade at reduced costs. The waterway, later known as the Trent and Mersey canal, connected the Trent south of Nottingham to the Bridgewater canal near Runcorn and thence to the River Mersey. National trade links would improve and international trade beckon, and branch canals would enable rural trades to expand as they merged with the Grand Trunk canal routes.

The scheme was finally approved by an Act of Parliament in 1765 and James Brindley was appointed as engineer. His untimely death in 1772 occurred before its completion in 1777 and the task was completed by his brother in law, Hugh Henshall. Meantime a body of interested businessmen formed what became known as the Company of Proprietors. The Company included the Duke of Bridgewater, Earl Gower, Thomas Anson, Matthew Boulton, Samuel Garbett, John Sneyd and Josiah Wedgwood. All had a vested interest.

The route of the canal ran from Wilden Ferry via Burton-on-Trent, Wychnor, Rugeley, Haywood, Sandon, Stone, Trentham and Stoke before leaving Staffordshire by the Harecastle tunnel. The canal emerged from the tunnel and made its way across the Cheshire Plain towards Runcorn and the Mersey. The cut, forming the canal was to be twelve feet wide and three feet deep and was intended to carry a barge seventy feet long and six feet wide, with a draft of two feet six inches. In the event the dimensions were adjusted to more practical measurements.

With a carrying capacity of twenty tons and a smooth, damage free passage it is easy to see why barge transport was welcomed by industry. Even more attractive was the saving on cost. Carrying by land, using the traditional mule and pannier, was running at nine shillings per ton for every ten miles covered. The arithmetic is simple enough. A twenty ton load taken from Cheddleton to Burslem would travel about ten miles at a cost of one hundred and eighty shillings - and there was no guarantee that breakages would not occur. By contrast, the cost of carriage by barge was two shillings and six pence per ton over the same distance.

Understandably, the Company of Proprietors were keen to expand the canal network. The Churnet Valley, with its long tradition of rural trade, had long suffered the hazards of road transportation. Villages such as Kingsley, Froghall, Oakamoor and Consall faced the task of the muddy and precarious journey along the bottom of the valley or the very steep exit routes that headed towards Cheadle, Ipstones and Whiston.

The idea of a local branch canal was met with enthusiasm by those who lived and worked in the valley. Less enthusiastic were those whose business would be affected by the new waterway. The first reference to a branch canal comes from Josiah Wedgwood, who in 1775 wrote to a Mr Bentley: *'They have enlisted me here in another navigation scheme, to effect a junction between Caldon Lime Quarries and our canal and Collieries. You know the Plan, I only mean that we are begun upon it in earnest'.*

On November 27th 1775, John Sparrow wrote to Charles Bill about the proposed canal: *'A Plan has long been in Agitation for extending a Branch of the Canal, from the Summit at Harecastle, to an inexhaustible fund of Limestone near Caldon in Staffordshire. Surveys have been made of various courses for this purpose, and at last a very eligible one has been discovered, the length of which is 19¹/4 miles. An accurate estimate has been made of the expense, which amounts to £23,126.'*

The survey referred to an envisaged route, *'From Cheddleton, a railed way could be made for the carriage of coal, stone and other goods from the canal to a place called Sharpcliffe. From there the canal could be continued to several lime works and limestone quarries at Cauldon.'*

The formal proposal was made on 12th February 1776 and a petition against the proposal followed immediately. On l9th March 1776, John Bagnall, Benjamin Yardley and William Adams, owners of water driven corn mills at Cheddleton, Milton and Bucknall and several landowners and farmers objected to the canal on the basis that it would have to be supplied from springs and rivulets which fed the rivers which drove their mills.

A revised proposal was placed before parliament on the 18th April 1776. This time the route was to continue from Cheddleton, via Consall to Froghall. From Froghall a railway would be made leading to the lime works at Caldon. Permission was approved by an Act of Parliament passed in May 1776.

The new route from the Trunk canal at Etruria to the Froghall termination, was a distance of 17¹/4 miles. An estimated cost was given of £23,000 plus a sum of £5,000 to be paid by colliery owners.

The tolls were set at 1¹/2 d per ton per mile for coal, stone, timber and other goods carried on the canal and railway, and a special toll of ¹/2d, per ton per mile

The busy wharf at
Cheddleton in the 1920s.

Harry Bold's shop, long
since closed and replaced by
a restaurant in the 1970s.
Courtesy of Roger Bold

for coal brought from mines in the parishes of Kingsley and Cheadle. The actual date that the canal opened for business is debated. Land was still being purchased in the Shelton area in 1777 and no toll receipts are recorded until 1778. An actual date of late 1778 coincides with the recorded tolls collected by Edward Sneyd. From Christmas 1778 until Christmas 1779 a sum of £896 passed to Mr Sneyd probably representing a figure of around 100,000 tons which indicates just how busy the canal was. Over a period of six months from the 14th June to the 27th December, the revenue produced from tonnage was £13,337.

An Act to extend the length of the canal from Froghall to Uttoxeter was passed on 6th June 1797 chiefly to carry coal from the Kingsley and Cheadle mines, to transport copper and brass from Oakamoor and Alton and to transport lime for agricultural use. The plans were opposed by the Earl of Shrewsbury who owned the Alton Wire Mill, and by the Cheadle Brass Company who leased the mill from the Earl. Once again the objections centred on the restriction of water supplies to local water mills. The Earl was not without influence and the project was delayed for several years.

A route that passed through the mill ponds was considered on the basis that the canal would leave the pond before reaching the wire mill. Agreement could still not be reached and consideration was given to the building of railways between the proposed canal at Froghall and the turnpike road at Stubwood.

In 1805, Matthew Brindley, manager of the Alton Wire Works, and a relative of James Brindley was instructed to *'pursue the line of the canal from Froghall to the Alton mills and, to examine whether the Navigation company make use of, or divert any streams of water belonging to the river Churnet, and to make reports accordingly.'* He appears to have ignored it completely.

The extension, in the meantime was still going ahead. No opposition remained between Froghall and Oakamoor and that section was completed by 1808. By early 1809 the canal had reached the outskirts of Alton. Agreement with the Earl of Shrewsbury was finally reached on the 13th March 1809. The agreement permitted the canal to pass through part of the millpond. In return, the Company of Proprietors agreed to construct a new weir and pond for the mill eighteen inches above the level of the original pond. The canal finally reached its destination at Uttoxeter in September 1811.

Uttoxeter celebrated. On the 20th September 1811 *The Times* reported that the news of the opening had been received in Uttoxeter with great demonstrations of joy. The Staffordshire Advertiser gave a full account:

`In the extensive basin lay two elegant pleasure boats for the use of the proprietors and their friends - with four or five other boats. The Prince Regent

boat took the lead and proceeded in good style to the beautiful cast iron aqueduct over the river Tean. After passing Rocester, where upwards of three hundred people belonging to Mr Bridden's cotton works attended, the boat arrived at two o'clock in the grand weir across the river Churnet at Crumpwood.'

THE LEEK BRANCH

Leek would have also found much to celebrate when the long awaited spur that terminated at Barnfields, close to Newcastle road, was finally completed.

The Leek branch of the Caldon Canal leaves the main route below Longsdon and after rising steadily through a series of locks, crosses the Main Caldon canal by means of the Hazelhurst Viaduct [1841] at Denford.

The scene today, with the Hollybush Inn close by, remains little changed from then. The Leek branch offers great tranquillity. Should you choose to walk along the towpath from Denford towards Leek, you will still encounter much the same scene enjoyed by our parents and grandparents. Even the buzzards are back and the wild flowers proliferate in the fields. As you approach Tunnel Pool in late spring the woods on your left are awash with bluebells.

On your right, amid the woodlands that cover the banks of the Churnet, can be seen the water tower that once supplied the local asylum - St Edward's Hospital. Constructed in the latter 19th century, it retains a place in the affections of Cheddleton people. The hospital was finally closed just a few years ago around the year 2000 when many of the wards were demolished. In their place, new 'quality' housing graces richly landscaped grounds, and only the water tower and main hospital remain looking down on the scene.

At Tunnel Pool, the occasional barge disturbs the fishermen as it turns around for its return journey. The canal continues for a mile or so. If you climb the hill you can follow the path towards the edge of the Barnfields Industrial Estate where the canal now ends. You can walk through the estate and follow the road to Wharf House close to the Newcastle Road and where the Focus DIY store now stands was once the old Leek canal basin.

As often happens, it looks like it will turn a full circle because now a feasibility study is underway to look at extending the Leek branch once again to the Barnfields Estate around the Cattle Market, along with a new Leek railway station from the Churnet Valley line. Glorious dreams indeed!

LIMESTONE AND RAILWAYS

The comment made by John Sparrow to Charles Bill regarding *'an inexhaustible fund of limestone'* near Cauldon was not too far wide of the mark. Even today, in the early 21st century, the cement company at Cauldon Lowe

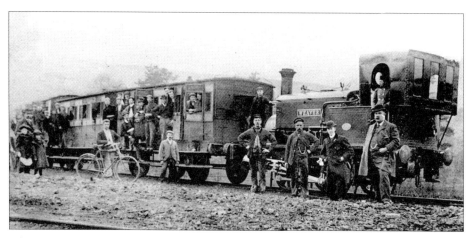

The Asylum train operated from Leekbrook Junction along the Asylum's private tramway, mainly delivering goods to the hospital although it also had a passenger car for visitors and inmates.

St Edward's Hospital, Cheddleton - the Asylum.

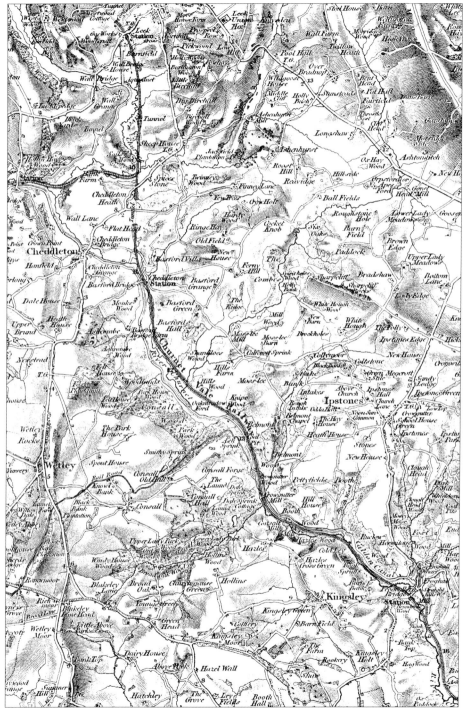

The Churnet valley line seen on the 1880s Ordnance Survey map.

continues to produce vast quantities of lime based products.

At the time of Sparrow's letter in 1775, the Cauldon Lowe lime quarries were owned by the Earl of Shrewsbury. When the canal was cut the Earl granted a long lease on the quarries to John Gilbert of Worley, Sampson Whieldon of Cauldon, George Smith of Eaves in Whiston and Richard Hill of Farley. This group called themselves the Caldon Lime Company. They also obtained leases on coal measures near to Froghall.

Other coal mines in the vicinity of Froghall were owned by Edward Leigh, Thomas Mytton and John Beech who each agreed to lend £5000 to the Canal Company to support the construction costs of a railway between Cauldon and Froghall. Meantime the canal's Company of Proprietors reached agreement with Thomas Gilbert, John Gilbert, Richard Hill, George Smith, Sampson Whieldon, Henry Copestake, Robert Bill and William Wooliscroft, all of whom were owners or leaseholders of limestone quarries in Cauldon.

The Company agreed to build a railway to carry limestone from Cauldon to the canal wharf at Froghall. A rate of 7d per ton was agreed upon for the limestone with the proviso that, in the event of failure to deliver the agreed tonnage, the Company could enter the quarries and take away what they wanted at a rate of 2d per ton. A minimum order of 100 tons was agreed, with 2d per ton being paid as a deposit. A final figure of between 600 and 1000 ton a month would be expected after five months.

Far from being a straight forward operation, the building of the railway between Cauldon quarries and Froghall wharf proved extremely difficult. Ultimately, and over many years, three railways were constructed, before a fourth reasonably safe and efficient route was secured.

The method of construction would have been similar in each case but with improvements brought about by experience and technology. Farey, in his review of the canals, noted that the plateway or railway was constructed with cast iron bars, spiked down upon wooden sleepers. The cost is given as about £1 per yard.

On a reasonably flat terrain or on a gentle slope the method of construction would probably have been adequate. But this route was '*very crooked, steep and uneven in its degree of declivity, in different parts*'. The builders of the original railway simply took a direct route that started where the canal ended and then ran on to Shirley Hollow before crossing the Garston to Foxt road and then across Shirley Common and on to Cauldon.

In 1783 the Company extended the canal by another 530 yards and this, in effect, made the first railway obsolete and a second railway had to be constructed. This time the railway headed towards Garston Wood before turning right towards Whiston. It then continued past Garston and Cotton Common towards Cauldon, a distance of just over three miles. At a meeting in 1785, the Company reported that a sum of £6,000 had been spent over the last two years, building warehouses and reservoirs and the forming of a new railway from Cauldon to Froghall. Even so, by 1790 further improvements were necessary and another £834 was spent on the railway.

In 1802 yet another Act of Parliament was approved. This time John Rennie was appointed as engineer, with instructions to '*alter the course of the railway from Froghall to Caldon*'. This third railway had a double line of flanged plateways, spiked to stone blocks. Five inclined planes were constructed to accommodate the rise of 649 feet. The line was completed in 1803 and was considered to be among the most complete of its kind in Britain.

The method of controlling the wagons demanded a degree of ingenuity. Each wagon could carry up to one and a half tons and, twelve full wagons plus twelve empty ones travelled the railway between the hours of 5.30am and 5.30pm each day. During a twelve hour period up to 270 tons of limestone were deposited at the Froghall wharf. Horses were used to haul the wagons across the flat terrain, with extra horses being used when coal was being carried.

A system of winding drums and chains, powered by steam engines, was installed at the end of each plane. A brake was attached to each pulley to limit the speed of the descent and was operated by the brake-man.

From the beginning of the Froghall plane the line ran for three quarters of a mile to the bottom of the Whiston plane and then from the beginning of the Whiston plane to the bottom of the Cotton plane. In each case pulleys and chains were used to control the movement of the wagons. The final stretch ran from the beginning of the Cotton plane, for a distance of one and three quarter miles, to the face of the Cauldon quarries.

The system, simple in engineering terms, worked well enough, although the steepness of the descents, especially at Froghall, put great strain on the mechanism. Rennie's railway ran until 1847, before more advanced technology led to its replacement with a fourth and final line. This time the line followed a more direct route and was worked entirely by mechanical power and cables.

Despite the growing popularity of the 'new' Churnet Valley Railway, the canal system competed favourably for the carriage of limestone for some while and it was not until 1920 that the Cauldon to Froghall railway finally closed. Spasmodic trade on the canal survived for a few more decades but reduced tonnage and growing competition, from road as well as rail, brought about its inevitable demise.

The canal could easily have slipped into terminal decline but after several years of neglect a new lease of life was provided by enthusiasts anxious to maintain our industrial heritage and a pleasant, less hectic way of life. With the help of British Waterways and volunteers, tow paths were repaired and locks and bridges renovated. Nowadays the diesel engine has replaced the horse and the narrow boats are pleasure-crafts, but the Caldon canal is still in use.

JAMES BRINDLEY 1716-1772

James Brindley, sometimes referred to as the 'Old Schemer', is remembered as the greatest of the canal engineers. The word genius is loosely applied but few would argue that Brindley was an engineer of extraordinary talent. He was not only a surveyor and designer of canal systems, he was also an accomplished engineer who could find a solution to any technical problem. He patented a steam engine boiler, worked on mobile water engines and repaired flint grinding machinery. He constructed a flint mill at Tunstall and is thought to have been involved in the construction of many others, including the Cheddleton mill.

Brindley's father married Susanna Bradbury and James junior was one of their seven children. The family had leanings towards non-conformist religion and the Quaker movement is apparent in their ancestry. The Quakers were great believers in equality and education and pioneered the art of learning. The Brindley children seem to have benefited from their education. His three brothers also left their mark. John became an important potter in Burslem and died a rich man. Joseph settled in Alton and prospered as the manager of the Alton Brass and Wire Works. Henry became a farmer and lived in Cheshire.

When James was ten, the family moved from Tunstead in Derbyshire and settled at Lowe Hill, near Leek, and in 1733, at the age of seventeen, James was apprenticed for seven years, as carpenter and millwright, to Abraham Bennet of Sutton, near Macclesfield. The term millwright had a more literal meaning at that time. Machinery was yet to benefit from the introduction of carbonised steel and was built with timber and iron, demanding the skills of a craftsman versed in the arts of both. Carpentry and engineering skills made the millwright a much sought after tradesman.

James proved to be a person of exceptional ability and was trusted by Bennet to complete the repairs to a paper mill on the River Dane When Abraham Bennet died, James was trusted enough by the family to run the business until it was wound up in 1742.

James now returned to Leek, where he took over the old and run down water mill on the junction of Mill Street and Abbey Green road. The mill was enlarged substantially, the machinery updated and the premises modernised. Whether or not he intended to remain in Leek and operate from his mill is difficult to say, but his skills were recognised and he was soon in great demand.

He now spent a great deal of time working throughout the Midlands and his work in the Potteries brought him into contact with Josiah Wedgwood. He inspected and overhauled pumps for Earl Gower and was later engaged by the Duke of Bridgewater to survey the Worsley to Manchester section of the Bridgewater canal. His work on the Bridgewater canal resulted in him acting as parliamentary witness in the Houses of Parliament.

Brindley's expertise was gaining him national recognition. It is said that his mode of dress, suited to his 'hands on' approach to work, and his Staffordshire dialect did little to enhance his prospects socially. Even so, his lack of pretentiousness and an ability to articulate the complexities endeared him to those eager to engage his talents. From 1760 onwards he was primarily involved in canal work but he still found time for other jobs. *The History of Cheddleton* (Ed. Robert Milner) carries a chapter attributed to Robert Copeland, who suggests that Brindley was the designer of the north mill at Cheddleton. Brindley's expertise in the grinding of flint and his proximity to Cheddleton would have made him an obvious candidate for the job.

He married in 1765, somewhat late in life, to Ann Henshall. The marriage was blessed with two daughters, Ann born in 1770 and Susanna in 1772. Susanna went on to marry John Bettington, a merchant from Bristol and they emigrated to Australia where their descendants amassed a fortune.

James now became involved in the building of the Grand Trunk Canal Scheme, a main canal artery into which all other canals would flow. For the businessmen of the 18th century it was a vision on a grand scale. Comments made about Brindley by his business associates illustrate very well the respect in which he was held. Josiah Wedgwood said, after a meeting of the Trent and Mersey Canal Company, *'Brindley was called upon to state his plans, brought them forward with such extraordinary lucidity of detail as to make them clear to the dullest intellect present.'*

A contemporary considering the complexities of building the Harecastle Tunnel wrote: *'Gentlemen, come to view our eighth wonder of the world, the subterraneous navigation, which is a cutting by the great Mr Brindley, who handles rocks as easily as you would handle plum pies, and makes the four elements subservient to his will. He is as plain a looking man as one of the boors of the Peak, or one of his own carters, but when he speaks all ears listen, and every mind is filled with wonder at the things he announces to be practicable.'*

Brindley's prodigious workload was to lead to his death. He was surveying the route of the Caldon canal and after being caught in a shower he spent the night at an inn in Ipstones where he is said to have slept in a damp bed. He caught a severe chill and returned to his home, Turnhurst Hall, where he took to

The Irwell viaduct - one of Brindley's early achievements.

The Brindley Mill in Leek and its water-wheel.

his bed. He was visited on a daily basis by his great friend, Josiah Wedgwood but within days the great engineer passed away. He died on 27th September 1772. Wedgwood was moved to say that Brindley's death *'will deprive us of a valued friend and the world of one of those great geniuses who seldom live to see justice done to their singular abilities, but must trust to future ages for that tribute of praise and fair fame they so greatly merit'*.

Perhaps the final tribute to James Brindley can be left to Erasmus Darwin:

> *So with strong arm immortal Brindley leads*
> *His long canals and parts the velvet meads*
> *Winding in lucid lines, the waiting mass*
> *Minds the firm rock, or loads the deep morass.*

> *While rising locks a thousand hills alarm,*
> *Flings o'er a thousand streams its silvery arm,*
> *Feeds the long vales, the redding woodland laves,*
> *And plenty, arts and commerce freight the waves.*

> *Nymphs, who erstwhile on Brindleys' early bier,*
> *On snow white bosoms shed the incessant tear,*
> *Adorn his tomb. Oh, raise the marble bust,*
> *Proclaim his honours and protect his dust.*

> *With urns inverted round the sacred shrine,*
> *Their Ozier-wreaths let weeping Naiads twine,*
> *While on the top mechanic Genius stands,*
> *Count the fleet waves and balance the sands.*

As an aside, the village of Sutton, near Macclesfield, has played host to two of the greatest men to have graced Leek and the Churnet Valley. Joshua Wardle also lived at Sutton and like Brindley served his apprenticeship nearby.

IRON WORKING

On the face of it, villages such as Consall, Froghall and Oakamoor are little more than rural backwaters but at the height of the industrial revolution they were anything but so. Hundreds, even thousands of men worked in the Churnet Valley and frequented the local villages. Iron ore was extracted over many centuries and copper, tin, lead and coal were also found in the valley. Each attracted itinerant workers who helped to shape the life and character of the villages. Ironstone was so abundant in places that it could be dug from the banks of the streams that ran through the wooded hillsides.

In its simplest form, the iron-age had existed for aeons. Man's ingenuity had enabled him to develop primitive ways to smelt and forge the metal extracted from the stone. Whether or not wrought iron was produced in the Churnet Valley during the Neolithic period is uncertain. Even suggestions that iron was being produced in the 11th century are difficult to substantiate but several sites in the valley contain slag heaps and the debris of iron production.

In its more primitive state, iron was produced in small amounts by the simplest of methods. Ironstone would be placed into a small heap and surrounded by a large fire. The fire would be sealed with turf and air holes inserted at intervals around the perimeter. The intensity of the fire cracked the stone and the iron smelted into irregular lumps which could be reheated en mass and formed into a single ingot.

By the 11th century a degree of sophistication existed. Stone floors, sometimes with a central pit, formed a solid hearth on which to build the fire. The molten iron ran into moulds - 'pigs'. Bellows made from animal hides helped the fire burn hotter and smelt the iron more efficiently. The slag or waste from the fire was raked away and discarded, and slag-heaps are much in evidence at Eastwall and at Mathers Wood near Farley. Herbert Chester, in his *The Iron Valley* quotes from the *Secunda Carta of Cheadle (The Sutherland Documents)*: '*the old mines of iron and my old forges with two or three other amenities*'. The document is dated 1290 and relates to a large parcel of land around Estewelle (Eastwall). In Mathers Wood, sometimes known as Smithe Wood or Colmore Wood, slag is found spread over an area of forty yards. It is believed that some of the slag was removed during the 16th century and reworked in a furnace that was built a few miles away at Oakamoor, noted on maps as Old Furnace.

Haematite fragments, discovered at Consall close to the River Churnet, are also found at Eastwall, so ironstone may have been taken from Consall to Eastwall. This fits in with the records of Dieulacres Abbey. In 1413 a monk from Dieulacres and eight armed men broke into the park of William Egerton of Cheddleton, and took by force from it stone called '*ernestone*', to the value of 100 shillings. William was Lord of the Manor and Consall was part of his estate.

Sister Mary Lawrence, in her transcripts of the *Chronicles of Croxden Abbey*, adds much to the story of medieval iron-working in the area. Timber and charcoal were in great demand at bloomery sites and the abbey woods were cut and burnt systematically, both to meet demand and to provide an income.

1291 'Our woods at Gybbe Ruydinges was burned'.

1309 'Our woods at Gybbes Ruydinges sold for 26 marks'.

1367 'Sold woods called Gybbe Ruydinges to Didon of Waterhouses for 19 marks and the underwood of Greatgates at 12 loads of charcoal for 20 pence, spread over 3 years brought 100 marks'.

As charcoal in large volume was almost exclusive to iron smelting, it takes little imagination to accept that iron making was a major activity in the Churnet Valley long before formal records began to appear.

By the end of the 15th century France was leading the way in iron production with a new two part method of manufacture. First, the iron was smelted in a 'blast' furnace and the molten metal run off as pig iron. The second process removed the carbon content by the use of a forge in two stages. Initially, the pig iron was reheated and then refined by hammering until the impurities had been removed - the 'finery' process - then the iron was reheated and put through the 'chafery' process where the iron was shaped into bars that were subsequently used by the iron workers and the blacksmiths to produce articles for agriculture and industry.

The first blast furnace in England was built in 1496 in Sussex. Within fifty years they were commonplace and South Staffordshire could boast many. The villages of Tipton, Smethwick and Birmingham spawned a multitude of cottage industries in what was later to become known as the Black Country where nail-making and chain-making occupied entire families. Stoke supplied huge amounts of iron to South Staffordshire.

Both forge and furnace used water power, whether to operate the bellows of the furnace or to raise the mighty drop hammers of the forge. Steam engines later began to offer an alternative but they did little to resolve the real problem facing iron production - the fuel used to heat the furnace. Charcoal burners were everywhere and large tracts of woodland disappeared as the demand for iron grew. Coppices were introduced in an effort to keep pace but it became a question of which would collapse first, the iron trade or the supply of charcoal. Almost in the nick of time, improved furnaces enabled first coal, then coke, to be used as the preferred fuel.

Ironically, the largest users of iron now became the railways who opened up the country and so introduced greater competition to the rural manufacturers. This and the development of improved steam engines would mean the end of the local water mills. Slowly the woodlands recovered as the scars of industry began to disappear and no longer does the Churnet Valley reverberate to the sound of the drop hammer or palls of smoke no longer hang over the villages of Consall and Oakamoor. The valley is silent once again.

Chapter Four
Consall and Consall Forge

INDUSTRIAL HAMLET

The years have failed to diminish the charm of this tiny hamlet. Despite the occasional intrusion of the 20th century it remains an oasis of calm as well as an insight into the industrial revolution. The traveller does not expect what lies beyond the junction off the Wetley Rocks road and winding rural lanes. Stone houses straddle the road and dairy farms are surrounded by ancient hedges.

For the most part the properties are of 17th century origin, although many of the larger homes have been altered during the 18th and 19th centuries. Long Meadow farmhouse is a typical 18th century example and Lower Farm and Middle Farm were originally built in the 17th century. Middle farmhouse appears to have been re-faced during the 19th century but a small carved head within the structure points to the 17th century. Lower farmhouse has late 19th century additions with timber framework on a sandstone plinth.

At nearby Lawn Farm the fields were once subject to the rigors of the industrial revolution, although little now remains of the coal shafts and engine house. In all, three coal mines and four iron mines were sunk, probably during the 18th century. The coal was low grade material from the Crabtree seam but it was good enough for use in the lime kilns or the furnaces of the iron forges. Transportation of the coal and iron was by plateways that led to Consall Forge or to the outskirts of Longton via the Consall plateway.

Coal mines, iron mines and stone quarries proliferated in the Churnet Valley and added to the output from the water mills, the forge and the slitting mill that stood on the banks of the river. Quarrying is evident in Coalpit Wood, Ash Sprink, Rough Knipe, Prices Cave, Crowgutter Wood, Consall Forge and more abundantly, in Wetley Rocks. Ash Sprink appears to have been the last one until after World War I. A plateway led to the Caldon canal.

The canal was the lifeline for local industry. It is difficult to appreciate just how busy the Consall area must have been at its peak. Many local houses would have extended hospitality to lodgers and the village school would have accommodated a rich diversity of pupils. The school broke the stone tradition of the Staffordshire Moorlands and was built of local bricks. The pretty three-roomed building must have been out of favour before the turn of the century as local pupils are recorded as attending the village school in Wetley Rocks. In

The village school at Consall, taken from an old plan.

1912 it was converted into a cottage at the behest of Mr Meakin.

Fortunes were made by those prepared to grasp the opportunity. Mary Podmore, in her article *The Quiet Village* tells of Captain Ironstone Smith who lived in the Old Hall towards the end of the 18th century. The Captain was not too worried about living cheek by jowl with industry and he made enough money from the mines on his land to build New Hall for his son. The name New Hall persists to this day although it is now over two hundred years old.

Mary Podmore tells of stone, quarried at Consall, being used to build the canal locks, and of the old brickworks that stood at the mouth of the valley using local clay for its bricks. A Cornishman named Bishop was one of the early pioneers who realised the extent of the iron ore in the valley and went into business extracting it. At its peak, thousands of tons per year were extracted as the industrial revolution mechanised what had gone on for centuries before.

In an indenture between William De Ipstones, Lord of Ipstones and John De Draycote, Lord of Draycote, John De Draycote is not to be disturbed by William '*in his woods and mines in Consale*' during his life. The indenture is witnessed by Robert de Lockwood, James de Draycote and John Berdmor and is dated 1399.

By the time Dr Robert Plot arrived in 1686 he was able to make specific reference to Consall in his *A Natural History of Staffordshire*. Plot describes a thriving industry:

'*....from the furnaces they bring their sows and pigs of iron when broken asunder, and into lengths, to the Forges, which are two sorts, but commonly (as at Consall) standing together under the same roof, one of which is called the*

Finery, the other the Chafery, they are both of them open hearths, upon which are placed great heaps of coal, which are blown by bellows like to those of the Furnaces, and compressed the same way, but nothing near so large.

In these two forges they give the sows and pigs several heats before they are perfectly wrought into bars .....the great Hammers raised by the motion of a water wheel, and first beat it into a thick square, which they call a half bloom. Then they put it into the Finery again for an hour, then bring it again to the same Hammer, where they work it into a bloom. Then brought to the Chafery, where after it has been heated for a quarter of an hour, it is also brought to the Hammer, and there beat quite out into a bar.'

Water-wheels in the Churnet Valley were commonplace although the use to which they were put was frequently changing. Corn grinding and flint grinding are examples. In Rocester, the monks used the power of the water wheel to operate their fulling mills, and in Alton, a paper mill and a wire mill depended on water power. In Oakamoor and in Consall the forges utilised the water wheel to raise the huge drop hammers for the shaping of wrought iron.

The water wheels, the forge and the slitting mill stood on the confluence of a stream that ran into the Churnet from the edge of Crowgutter wood. A short distance away a second mill stood on the banks of the Churnet at Hazelwood. The Crowgutter mill was the more substantial and being upstream controlled the flow of water. To compensate the mill at Hazelwood a weir was constructed at Consall Forge. The weir is still much in evidence although both mills have all but disappeared. The size of the main mill is indicative of just how important Consall was to the iron industry.

John Leigh of Consall put the estate up for sale in 1841. At the time the colliery was referred to as Chase Colliery and the sale details noted that the Railway (N.S. RAILWAY 1815) passes close to the pits sunk for working coal *.....at present no coal has been worked for sale, but merely for use of the estate and lime kilns.*

Of greater importance is Lot 4:

THE CONSALL FLINT MILLS

'These important and well known mills are situated under the wooded hills on the eastern side of the Consall Hall domain on the banks of the Trent and Mersey canal, connecting them with the sea. They are distinguished as the Upper and Lower Consall Mills'.

The catalogue states that *'the wheels have a constant supply of spring water for the washing of pottery materials' and that 'immense sums have been*

*expended in planning and completing these mills (especially the Upper Mill)
with all their valuable and admirable machinery and appendages, on the most
improved principles'.*

The buildings housed three water wheels of iron and two of them are
described as *'lately new'*, thirty feet in diameter and nine feet wide. The mills,
in all, worked 17 or 18 pans producing 300 to 350 tons of slops per week (slops
were liquid used in pottery industry). The size of the complex is given as 18
acres of land with several cottages with gardens for the mill men, and all the
necessary erections as *'Kilns, Arks, Stabling etc'*. An annual profit of at least
£3,000 to £4,000 was anticipated.

When Mary Podmore wrote about Consall in the 1950s one of the old
wheels was still working. A steam engine, a rare specimen of engineering and
a forerunner to Watt's steam engine boiler, is said to have been sent to the
Loughborough College Museum. Provisional enquiries reveal that the location
of this Newcomen boiler is unknown.

The Podmores were very much involved in the engineering side of the
pottery industry. Innovative and skillful, they were worthy successors to the
pioneers that dominated early industry in the Churnet Valley.

A field trip organised by the University of Keele in 1984-1985 confirmed
much of what is known about the Consall Forge area and added to our
knowledge. Reference to Crowgutter Mill is made on a map dated 1899,
although it is thought to precede that date by at least eighty years. No reference
to Crowgutter mill is found on the William Yates map of 1775, leading to the
conclusion that the mill was built shortly after the completion of the Caldon
canal. The mill had fallen into a state of disrepair by the end of the 19th century
but was put back into production in the 1930s by the Podmore family. Its finale
came in 1947 when a severe frost cracked the pipe that fed the turbine and it
was deemed uneconomical to repair it.

Rex Wailes made a study in 1967 and wrote about Crowgutter Mill:

*'Gilkes' Impulse turbine, the only impulse turbine in Staffordshire as far as
is known. The water came in a pipe about 10 inch diameter from a reservoir at
a much higher level, and was delivered at great pressure, hence the jet type
impulse engine. The drive was taken from the turbine by a flat belt onto a line
shaft with belt drives to cylinders and to a stone crusher'.*

The Consall mills complex was housed on a strip of flat meadow land
several hundred yards down stream from the Forge. It was a substantial
operation, used primarily for the slitting mills, where iron from the forge was
shaped into bars of various lengths and sizes. Plans of the mills show a water

The 'Devil's staircase' is still there at Consall Forge behind the Black Lion and leads to Belmont Pools.

The Devil's Staircase, Consall, Leek.

Below: The platform at Consall station perched above the Caldon canal.

wheel, numerous kilns, the factory buildings and workshops for the tradesmen such as the Smithy and the Carpenter's shop. Next to the Carpenter's shop stood the Superintendent's house, indicating that along with his pay went the privilege of living on the premises. Although there is no evidence, a railway between the forge and the mills is a reasonable assumption as the iron produced at the forge would need to be transported several hundred yards to the slitting mills.

The reference to a water wheel could mean that at least part of the site was occupied previously, although, from the way that the factory buildings follow the line of the canal, it is reasonable to assume that the main period of activity followed the construction of the canal in 1778.

Turning once again to the University of Keele and Rex Wailes we receive confirmation that local mills were converted to flint grinding when the iron trade began to flounder:

'Converted into a flint mill in the second half of the 18th century, and became important when the Caldon canal was cut. At this point the River Churnet, which powers the mill, flows almost entirely in the canal. There were three water-wheels (high breast) named Jack and Jill and Old Bill, 28ft diameter by 11ft wide, with buckets 1ft 8in deep and 2ft 1in on the curve. They ran with about 25ft of fall. They had cast iron shrouds and rings and three sets of twelve oak arms. One of the shafts was of steel forged in Belgium, 15in square by 30ft long. A 15ft diameter pit wheel of cast iron was cast in halves. Each wheel drove 4 pans, 2 overdrift and 2 underdrift.

In 1851 the mills were rebuilt and a new section added containing turbines, which had been exhibited at the 1851 Exhibition by W. Gunter of Oldham, later absorbed by Gilbert Gilkes and Gordon of Kendal. There were, at one time, sixteen 14ft pans absorbing 220 horse-power, four on each wheel and four on the turbine, and at one time a smaller turbine generated all the electric power. Now the turbine drives three modern ball mills with an incredibly noisy gear. There is a haystack boiler in the roof, now used as a water tank and leaking badly, and the older part of the mill is of stone; the floors are arched and of brick with cast iron beams and stanchions'.

Of the Forge itself, no trace remains; although records and maps indicate the site and a number of cottages plus a methodist chapel and the Forge Inn. The map shows the 'old forge' in 1841. Superimposed on the same map are the buildings recorded on plans and documents held in the Stafford Records office.

The forge was in great demand and the owners formed a business alliance with other ironmasters to ensure continuity of work. In 1689, Henry Glover,

Another view of the Black Lion, probably 1930s.

The Churnet and the Caldon canal running together alongside the railway
beyond Consall Forge and before Froghall.

The Black Lion and canal bridge at Consall seen in the 1970s. The Caldon canal and Churnet
are running together here before Consall Forge where they divide and go their own ways.

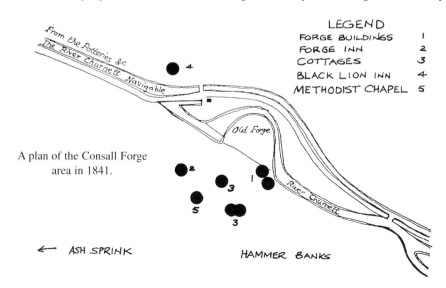

LEGEND

FORGE BUILDINGS	1
FORGE INN	2
COTTAGES	3
BLACK LION INN	4
METHODIST CHAPEL	5

A plan of the Consall Forge
area in 1841.

brother in law of Thomas Foley, was a well-known ironmaster in North Staffordshire with an interest in the Meir Heath furnaces, the forge and slitting mill at Oakwall moor (Oakamoor) and the forge and the slitting mills at Consall.

Two points of interest arise from the records relating to Henry Glover: Consall was used as a slitting mill at least a hundred years before the Caldon canal was cut, and iron was transferred from Consall to Meir Heath for smelting at the Foley works via a tramway. J.D. Johnstone, tracing the origins of the Consall plate-way points to the early 19th century, but it would seem that the route may well have been travelled before.

It is also worth noting that in addition to the prominent lime kilns by the Black Lion Inn, other lime kilns were in regular use. Lime kilns are recorded in Chase Wood to the north end of Consall Forge, on the banks of the Churnet. A plate-way carried the lime produced by the two kilns to the top of the wood. To the south east of the kilns a shaft was sunk for the extraction of iron stone.

There are also the traces of an ancient roadway or mule track out of the valley. This long forgotten way left the valley at a point behind where the Black Lion Inn now stands, probably in Crowgutter wood, and passed through Rough Knipe and below Prices Cave before winding round to the Belmont road en route to Ipstones or Cheddleton.

To gain some idea of the size of the Consall Estate we need look no further than the sale details of 1841 and 1848 when the affairs of John Leigh were being brought to a conclusion. At the time of the sale the Cheddleton Flint Mills are included in the Consall estate. The sale particulars refer to the mansion of Consall Hall with 1400 acres enclosed within a ring fence that encompassed walled gardens, ornamental waters and richly wooded park grounds. Also included were several farms, the village of Consall and plantations plus numerous cottages and dwellings. The Hall is described:

Dining room, drawing room, study or breakfast room, housekeeper's and butler's room, numerous bedrooms, large kitchen, scullery, dairy and other domestic offices with capital ale and wine cellar.

The number of inhabitants is difficult to ascertain, because of the movement of labour. In Whites Directory of 1851, Consall is described as a small village of 180 souls belonging to John Leigh and C.S.Smith, the latter being resident at the Hall. The main inhabitants are listed.

Chas. S. Smith	Hall
Thomas Fernihough	Wheelwright
William Wood	Millwright

Farmers (most likely tenant farmers):

Joseph Ball, Charles Booth, John W. Bowler, Thomas Corbitchley, William Corbitchley, Joshua Dale, William Fernihough, Ralph Hammond, Thomas Raines, Francis Stubbs and Charles Withington who was also the road surveyor.

Were the residents of Consall Forge included in the total? What seems strange is the omission of the landlords of the Black Lion and the Forge Inn and the names of the ironmasters, all important individuals. But Consall Valley industry was in its final fling. The affair with the Valley's mineral wealth had lasted for centuries and numerous suitors had played their part, with many companies set up to extract ironstone and coal, but now the compilers of the gazetters found little of interest, or profit, to include in their lists.

But miners, or Raddle men, were still in abundance, employed by the mineowners and ironmasters who had followed in the footsteps of William Bishop. Bishop came from Cornwall and settled in Kingsley around 1810 and he was responsible for the regeneration of interest in mining in the Churnet Valley. Many new businesses sprang up, land rights were claimed and long standing mineral rights, previously dormant, were given a new lease of life.

James Beech, Lord of the Manor of Kingsley, held land on the west side of the Churnet that bordered Dalesprink. Beech also owned land in the lower Mosey Moor valley near to Hermitage Farm and Ruelow Wood.

Adjacent, was the land of Captain Sergison Smith of Consall New Hall who held the mineral rights of much of the Consall estate.

Across the river, the former home of the Sneyd family, Belmont Hall was occupied by Mr J.G. Binns who was equally determined to benefit from the ironstone that lay beneath the Belmont estate.

Bordering the Belmont estate, the Ipstones Park area ran from Clough Head to Black Bank and was owned by fifteen farmers. They were quick to re-establish rights granted in 1649 to share the manorial benefits. These ancient rights caused endless problems as contractors sought to lease land from fifteen landlords, and with the problems of encroachment, trespass and way-leave it is easy to see why the lawyers were the only ones to really make money.

The Froghall Iron Ore Company was established to exploit the mineral wealth beneath Paddock Farm in Ipstones. In 1854, Robert Massey leased to Edward Hambly and partners the iron and coal under his land for a royalty of one shilling per ton for ironstone and sixpence per ton for coal. Later on the partners are named as Henry Onions Firmstone of Dudley, Edmund Hambly from Cornwall, Samuel Holden Blackwell of Dudley and Thomas Deyton Clare. In 1857 the lease was extended to a further 150 acres in Ipstones and granted for twenty-one years from 1856 until 1877.

Consall Minerals Ltd had offices in London - perhaps why the access bridge they built over the Churnet was called London Bridge.

Churnet Valley Iron Ore Company covered the area around Belmont and Crowgutter Wood, the area where William Bishop made his forays into the seams of ironstone. Jonathan George Binns was shrewd enough to lease from the Sneyds not only Belmont Hall but also the mineral rights of the estate and he became one of the most active ironstone men in the valley. Binns controlled the enterprises from Belmont and Crowgutter Wood to Booths and Hill House lands, plus part of the Mosey Moor area.

Binns allowed access to groups of miners, either directly or through his agent, Mr Ward. In 1862 Messrs Hargreaves and Hammond worked the Crowgutter area. Binns was eventually joined by the Dawes brothers, William and George, ironmasters from South Staffordshire, who brought capital that was used for sinking shafts and laying tramways. In Belmont greater emphasis was laid on transportation and from 1855 the carrying of ironstone to the canal and the railway became even more beneficial to them than the mining.

THE CONSALL PLATEWAY

There is much speculation about the Consall plate-way and many articles about it. Mr J.D. Johnstone of Werrington is credited with much of what follows:

The plateway, or tramway, was built early in the 19th century to transport metal ore from the mines at Mixon on Morridge and lime and limestone from Consall to Lane End on the outskirts of Longton, about seven or eight miles away. Coal, ironstone and quarried stone were all in demand and were all probably carried, especially goods destined for the potteries.

At the time of Johnstone's research in the 1950s, the track was traceable for more than half its length - levels, embankments, cuttings, stone gate posts, stone sleepers and sleeper depressions. The track began by the lime kilns on the banks of the canal and headed north through Ash Sprink and Chase Wood. After 3/4 mile, by some old kilns, it ascended through the woods to reach a height of two hundred feet as it entered Smithy Sprinks. It left the wood at Smithy Pool and then passed below Consall Old Hall, skirting the fish ponds and gardens constructed for Mr Meakin of Consall New Hall.

The track now crossed the culvert that fed the fish ponds and curved just below Lower Farm with its attractive black and white house. A further sweep took the track to Knowl Bank Farm and on towards Black Bank plantation and the road to Wetley Rocks. At this point, Johnstone notes a passing place and a Smithy. One of the cowsheds at the farm is built largely from the split stone sleepers that were used to support the track.

From Black Bank the track ran west to Tunnel Farm where it passed under the Wetley Rocks to Cheadle road. At Tunnel Farm there was a wharf and one of the rooms in the farm was used as an office. Interestingly, the wharf bears the same mason's marks as the lime kilns at Consall Forge.

At this point the plateway had reached a height of 863ft and ran along the shoulder of Rangemoor. In the 1950s, sleepers were still in place on the farm track that led to Lime Wharf Bank on the Cellarhead to Cheadle road, where the wharf stood. Contrary to held opinion the plateway did not end at Lime Wharf, it was only a terminus where another plate-way from Foxfield Colliery joined it, travelling from Dilhorne. The line crossed the road and entered a field to the north of March Lane, at the far end of which it took a westerly course towards Hands Farm, then diverted south west and passed below Mount Pleasant Farm.

Continuing along an embankment near to Grove Farm, the track passed just beyond the farm buildings and continued parallel to the main road past Ridgefields, Foxhearth House and Old Cat Gut Farm. To the south of Old Cat Gut it diverted from the present main road, crossed the old road to Windycot, and then ran across the large field behind Moorville Hall to emerge in the wood known as Cresswells Piece. A map dated 1840 of Weston Manor shows this as three fields, one called Railway Field.

From the wood, the plateway crossed Sheepwash Lane and then continued over open ground to Green Lane - part of the old saltway that ran from Salters Lane in Werrington to Salters Well near Bagnall.

From Green Lane the track curved on a large embankment towards the River Blythe, crossed a bridge, continued across Little Blythe Farm to Roughcote Lane and onto Blythe House land. For a short distance the line ran alongside the main road before negotiating a brook and curving to the west of the high ground above Bolton Gate Farmhouse. It crossed the main road at Little Weston (behind Weston Coyney Post Office), crossed the Bucknall road and passed through the fields to the west to a terminus on Weston Coyney Road. Housing development in Weston Coyney between 1850 and 1950 obliterated all traces of the line between here and its final destination in Longton.

Phillip's and Hutching's map of Staffordshire, 1832, shows the line only as far as Lime Wharf Bank and the Ordnance Survey map of 1835 shows it as far as Cresswells Piece.

Johnstone spoke to local people whose families had been around for generations and concluded that the line was not in use after 1868 - not surprising since the Churnet Valley line of the North Staffordshire Railway from 1850 became the main route for local industry.

Chapter Five
Froghall

FROGHALL WHARF

A strange little place! On the one hand it seems to have very little going for it. On the other hand it has everything. It offers peace and tranquillity, pleasant walks and industrial heritage. Wildflowers bloom everywhere and wildlife flourishes in the secluded woodlands.

But, like other hamlets in the valley, Froghall was a different place during the industrial revolution. The canal wharf, the numerous railways, the lime kilns and brick kilns, and later, the Churnet Valley Railway and Thomas Bolton's, all made Froghall a thriving industrial community. In earlier times the water mills were the site of a busy, but less frantic, industrial way of life.

The stories of the railways to the lime quarries of Cauldon Lowe and the cutting of the canal are told on previous pages but there is still more to be told.

On the Kingsley to Whiston road (A52) a bridge of sorts that straddled the river was replaced by the fine stone bridge that now carries the heavy lorries towards the sand quarries at Whiston Eaves. Visitors would do well to examine the 18th and 19th century stone work of this splendid double bridge across both the river and the railway lines. The Department of the Environment describes it thus:

'....*the river bridge has wide elliptical arches to low imposts and roll mouldings at carriage way level'*. The continuation of the bridge over the railway lines is '....*hatched with higher impost and parapet level and smaller elliptical arch ....an early 19th century farm house with rendered brick-work, tiled roof, end stacks in a T-shaped plan encompassing two storeys, four windows to the front and a set back wing, the central entrance having a cornice on moulded architraves. The house is possibly connected with the canal because of its close proximity to the wharf.'*

A much earlier reference to a house appears in a conveyance relating to John Beardmore, whose mansion is referred to as Froghall in Whiston. Dated 1612 it is drawn up by Nikolls and Hunte, solicitors, of Shrewsbury. John names his heir apparent as Thomas Goodanter, who receives several cottages in the Kingsley area plus land, meadows and buildings in and around the Whiston area. Also included in the conveyance are two water mills at Ipstones. Beardmore may well have had been involved in iron smelting as well.

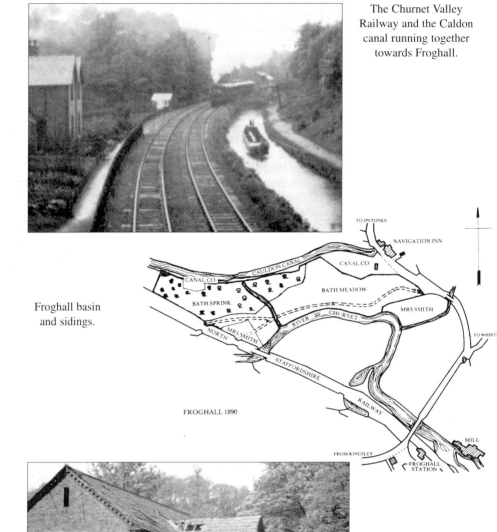

The Churnet Valley
Railway and the Caldon
canal running together
towards Froghall.

Froghall basin
and sidings.

FROGHALL 1890

Froghall wharf.

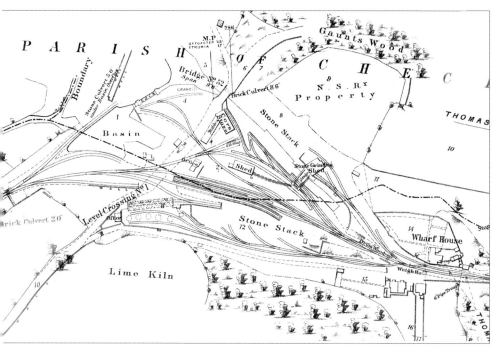

From an estate map c 1890.

The old Froghall station, now restored and rebuilt by the Churnet Valley Railway.

Kelly's directory of 1896 lists fourteen names:

Private Residents:
John Birch, Joseph Birch, Thomas Birch, William Birch, Rev. W. Musson Kelley
                                                    (Primitive Methodist)
Commercial Residents:
Joseph Alcock. Wharfinger and Agent. Goods department of the N.S.Railway &
                                                    Canal Co.
George Beavans. Farmer.
John Birch & Sons. Paint and Colour Manufacturer.
Bowers and Thorley. Lime burners and Merchants.
Thomas Bolton & Sons. Brass and Copper Works.
Froghall Stone Crushing Co. Henry Eaton, Manager.
William Harris. Grocer - Post Office.
John Lane. Shopkeeper.
Eliza Salt. Railway Hotel.

The Birch family were paint and colour manufacturers but they had more widespread interests. The Dane Bridge cotton mill closed prior to 1861 and was re-opened in the 1870s by John Birch, described as owner of a dye-works at Froghall and a carpet manufactory at Wildboarclough in Prestbury. In 1876, his son, Joseph, used the Dane Bridge Mill to make colour for the silk trade.

The Froghall Water Mill is thought to have been a two storey block. The ground floor was stone, and brick was used for the upper storey - perhaps a later addition. The entrance is a stone addition with the date 1825 carved into the keystone that formed the arch, probably when the lease changed hands in 1816. Documents from 1833 refer to the mill as '*a well accustomed water corn mill, in complete repair, having been erected a few years only, with drying kiln attached ....working five pairs of stones and having, both in winter and summer, a constant supply and large fall of water from the river Churnet*'.

Later, the construction of the Tittesworth reservoir interfered with the flow of water and from that time supplementary electricity was required. The grinding of corn had long since been abandoned and the mills have been used for colour and paint manufacturing. Materials consisted of manganese oxide, limestone from Cauldon and red oxide from around the Cherry Eye bridge area. They supplied colours for the pottery and silk dyeing industries, oxides for brick and tile makers, and whiting for agriculture.

The mechanism of the mill consisted of two undershot wheels. One wheel is thought to have been almost 16ft in diameter and 8 ft wide with three sets of eight arms carrying oversize buckets 10ft 9in wide. Transfer of power was by means of bevel gears and lay shafts that operated the two grinding pans.

Another wheel was 12ft in diameter and 4ft 4in wide. The head-race for the two smaller wheels passed over the tail-race of the larger wheel.

Once the main drive was in place, bevel gears, shafts and belt drives could transfer power almost anywhere. Pans could be added or removed with relative ease. The sketch plan illustrates the versatility of the mill. The details are taken from a fire insurance document and refer to the time when the mill was being used as a colour mill in 1898.

The mill ran spasmodically until the 1960s, then closed with the occasional resurgence - black smelt was ground there in 1995. Currently it is a scrapyard.

FIRE INSURANCE INVENTORY FROGHALL COLOUR MILL 1898.
(Former Corn Mill and Water Mill)

1. Smiths Shop and Brick-Hearth.

2. Lower or new colour mill. Three grinding pans and one crushing pan. Both grind iron ore and ochre in water. Smaller mill for grinding colours in oil - not used. One pair of millstones. One drying kiln.

3. Ground floor. Store for dried colours. First floor. Two pans of old mill stones, now used for grinding colours. Wire. One dressing machine.

   Second floor. Old Garner. One room now used for lumber. Old or middle mill. Old grinding mill now used for colour grinding in water. Large grinding pan or mortar mill and grinding pan.

3A. Timber-built store shed.

4. Old whitening mill or top mill for grinding ochre and colours in water. Four large iron grinding pans and potters slip press.

5. Drying kiln.

6. Old drying place for sand, limestone and whitening.

7. Greenhouse.

8. Timber weighing machine shed.

9. Colour drying shed and small slip kiln.

10. Lumber and engine oil.

11. Stable.

12. Piggery.

13. Cow shed with hay loft above.

14. Dwelling.

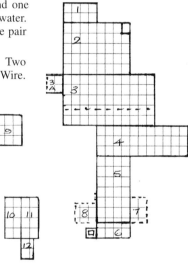

Sketch layout of
Froghall Colour Mill
1898
Insurance value
£2090

Details & sketch plan courtesy of
R. Sherlock, Staffs CC Historical Environmental Records

The Froghall Iron Ore Co is mentioned elsewhere. It appears there were also two brickworks and a 'Cupola' mill. The Cupola mill may owe its existence to the early attempts to smelt lead although its most positive reference is in 1812 when it was used for grinding flint. It merited its own tramway to Froghall wharf. The ordnance survey map of 1880 shows a brick kiln close to the wharf with a chimney stack which suggests a down draught kiln. A brickyard is recorded on the site that was taken over by Thomas Bolton's and another one is recorded further to the north on the road to Moseymoor wood.

There was also a gasworks that had a short but productive life and at one time was managed by a Mr Frost, the landlord of the Railway Inn. The works operated in conjunction with the Cheadle Gas Works and the two were connected by means of a pipeline that lay in a trench alongside the main road. The Froghall Gas Works consisted of three blocks of retorts that were operated continually on a three shift basis. Coal was brought by rail to the sidings originally installed by the Birch family. The coal fired furnaces produced a soft coke that was sold locally for domestic use and in the local churches. Gas was distributed to local villages including Oakamoor, Alton, Kingsley, Kingsley Holt, Whiston, Foxt and Ipstones. The end of production came when North Sea gas made small independent gas works unviable.

Add to all these the work at the canal wharf and the railway station and you begin to see just how busy Froghall was. The day book of the Limestone Works in 1885 lists over one hundred employees, including labourers, miners, drillers, wagon loaders and railway truck loaders. For a six day week, wages varied from 1s 4d to 4/- a day.

But dwarfing all these small industries in the Churnet Valley, were the giants of Thomas Bolton's (previously Cheadle Brassworks) at Oakamoor and Froghall, and Brittain's Paper Mills at Cheddleton, between them providing work for 2000-3000 people and exporting their products all over the world.

THOMAS BOLTON & SON LTD, FROGHALL

From the Autumn Edition 1936 Bolton News:

CHANGING SURROUNDINGS

The closing of the Clinkem siding .....is a fitting moment to recall activities in this area over the last hundred years. Prior to 1837 the Clinkem siding extended under a small humped back bridge at the foot of Whiston Bank. This was then a picturesque area with a huge row of poplars fronting the present Technical Dept, and a tiny row of cottages protruding into the roadway between the bridge and the Chapel. The roads were narrow and pleasant meadows surrounded the river where the Copper and Extrusion Depts now stand.

Thomas Bolton's Froghall works.

Thos. Bolton's, Froghall.

The gasworks at Froghall in a Churnet flood.
Courtesy of Mrs C.M. Chester

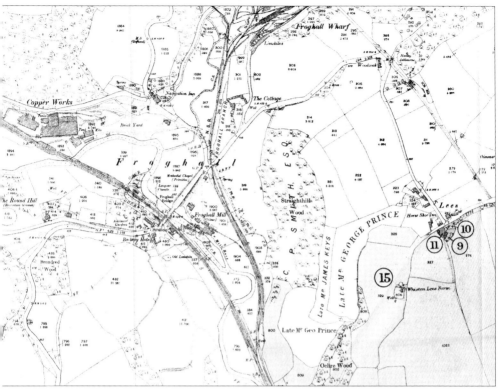

Ordnance survey map c. 1890.

Pushing copper scrap by hand into a refinery furnace at Bolton's, 1930s. No protection for head, eyes or hands with hot metal everywhere! Such practices hardly changed until the 1980s.

The sidings continued to the natural basin between the lime kilns and the canal. Here there were loading bays, both for rail and waterway, which handled limestone brought from the Caldon quarries by the old inclined ropeways. These railways depended upon heavily loaded down-coming trucks hauling empties to the top by an endless rope.

Some 50 or more years ago the basin was a scene of bustling activity with limestone being broken into ballast grades by a large gang of men: here too the limestone was burnt into agricultural lime. On the other side of the canal brickmaking was practised and further into the valley, between Foxt and Ipstones, coal was mined from galleries running into the valley sides. Most of the coal needed by the Company during the 1914-18 war was obtained from this site.

Some distance away, a colour mill, named the Cupola, ground stone and ceramic materials by water power. From the name it is likely that materials were fired in the Cupola during the process. The photograph taken in 1914, shows the great-grandparents of Mr R.P. Shaw, Chief Work Study Engineer, standing by the old water-wheel.

On the same page is a picture of Bolton's first car, registration number A51 and purchased in 1898. The car was passed down to various directors over the years who were expected to care for this symbol of British engineering. It was manufactured by Hercules Motor Waggon Company, Levershulme, Manchester.

The story of the arrival of the Bolton's in North Staffordshire is to be found in the pages relating to Oakamoor. The 'new' factory at Froghall was planned as a result of the growing demand for high conductivity copper and it was Bolton's first purpose-built factory. It was a greenfield site, away from the smoke and grime of the Oakamoor factory, but close enough to be controlled by the family. An agreement was reached with the Beech family for the purchase of two pieces of land, Bath Sprink and Bath Meadow, between the Caldon canal, the River Churnet and the North Staffordshire Railway.

The freehold of the site was purchased in July 1890 for £600. The Beech family, anxious to avoid the air pollution that enveloped Oakamoor, included in the agreement a stipulation that there should be *'no smoke or vapour injurious to vegetation on any land comprised in the indenture... and that no noxious refuse or other injurious substances shall be discharged into the River Churnet from the premises'*. They were ahead of their time - and much too hopeful!

By 1891 the first batch of electrolytic bar was cast at Froghall and taken to Oakamoor to be drawn down and tested. The results were excellent. Frank Bolton decided to double the capacity of the factory immediately. Two new engines and four dynamos were installed and within a few years Froghall had a monthly capacity of 700 tons of copper.

The Cupola Mill, and right, the water-wheel to the Cupola, in 1914.

The first Bolton's car, a Hercules, registration number A51 .

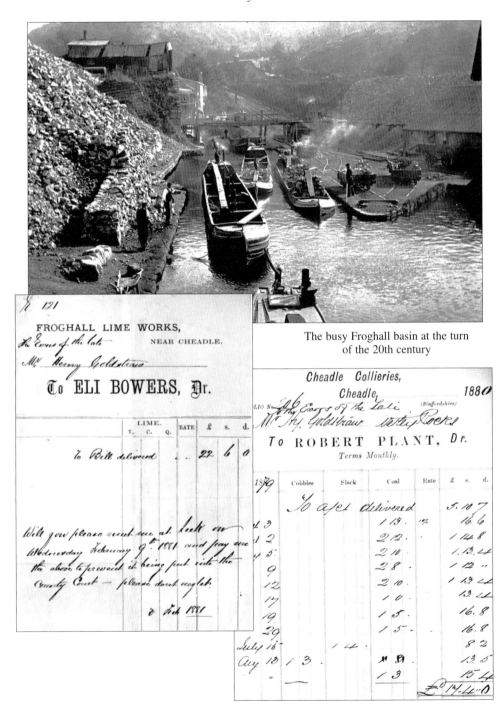

The busy Froghall basin at the turn
of the 20th century

Many villages just away from the Churnet saw their populations mainly employed in the factories and mines of the Valley, or in the Cheadle coalfields. Ipstones, Foxt and Kingsley were such. Ipstones was by the 1900s a busy working-class village and hundreds of workmen made their way down to Froghall every day.

A map of the early 1900s showing the area from just above Froghall to Ipstones.

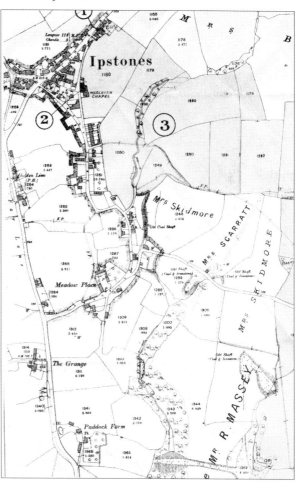

The Shawe at Kingsley was the home of the Lords of the Manor of Kingsley. In the 1800s it was the home of the Beech's who feature significantly in the story of industry around Consall and Froghall, as both landowners and entrepreneurs.

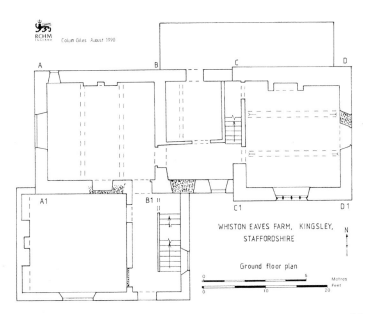

A plan of Whiston Eaves Farm, part of a report for WBB Minerals prior to demolition 1960s.

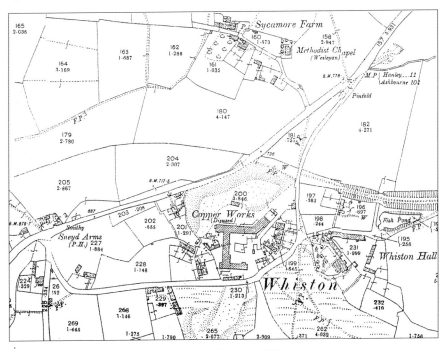

Ordnance Survey c 1890

Chapter Six
Whiston

INDUSTRIAL VILLAGE

The fortunes of Whiston have always revolved around its proximity to the Churnet and later the canal beside it. Although it does not merit its own entry in the Domesday book, Whiston is included in the entry for the Abbey of St Mary at Burton on Trent, indicating that it was part of the demesne lands belonging to the Abbey: *Belonged to Nawan. There is 1 hide, there is land for 1 plough. This is there with 1 Villan and 2 Bordars. It is worth 4s.*

Neolithic artefacts and stone age remnants all indicate that the area was familiar to iron age and even stone age man. Ancient greenways and tracks were used long before the familiar surfaced roads of today. An original track would surely have passed through the village before the road that now passes the Sneyd Arms, en-route to Froghall. The road to Oakamoor past Whiston Eaves and Crowtrees Farm would have been a greenway across the Plane. A track on the right, a short distance away from the village, led to Whiston Grange, probably belonging to Burton monastery prior to 1538.

Whiston Eaves, or just Eaves as it once was, has been much affected by extraction of silica sand. The road is, in places, a narrow arterial ribbon with a precipice on each side. The value of local stone and sand had long been recognised but was not really exploited until the 1950s when a landowner, Thomas Cooper, began to earn a living by extracting stone and sand from the Moneystone area. Thomas Cooper's mother, Millicent, had inherited the Whiston Hall estate from the Keys family. The quality, and the value, of the silica sand turned a rural backwater into a busy industrial enterprise.

British Industrial Sands purchased the farms belonging to the Smiths of Whiston Eaves in about 1959 and began to extract the sand in earnest. Tenanted farms that had existed for generations were put under threat. To buy or to move out became the question. Inevitably, many disappeared. Rakes Edge, an 18th century farm that had once benefited from the coal measures within its confines, failed to survive, the only evidence of its existence a name on a map and a single stone barn. Also gone is Whiston Eaves Hall and most of the nearby farm.

W.B.B. Minerals arranged for a full and detailed archaeological report on Whiston Hall farm and the farm buildings before their demise and the following are extracts from this with their kind permission:

The farmhouse has been subjected to several programmes of alteration and extension coupled with internal modifications and refenestration over a period which spans at least the 17th to 20th centuries ...there are indications that a timber-framed hall occupied the Site in the later middle ages... The timber-framed hall would appear to have still been in use when the east, cross-wing was constructed in stone in the 17th century... The present door on the eastern elevation has been chopped through an earlier window. The only access to this cross-wing would therefore have been through the hall.

The west cross-wing is of a similar date to the east, and its construction gave the building a fashionable symmetrical façade... The general quality of the stone work coupled with architectural detail such as corbelled kneelers, chamfered mullions and reveals, a ball finial (probably originally mirrored on the west cross-wing) and, inside, quarter round beams with decorated 'end stops' suggests that the house was occupied by a member of the gentry.

The structure was radically altered, probably in the 18th century. The west cross-wing would appear to have been demolished to ground level. Some of the stone was employed in the rebuilding of the rear elevations, but the majority was probably used for the front elevation. The upper two thirds of the rear elevation are of larger, square dressed blocks of different stone type and are more regularly coursed than in the earlier structure. A third storey was included in the new structure and the height of the ground floor room was increased considerably, probably to reflect the change in fashion and to create a new parlour or withdrawing room. Sooting and heat damage of the stone work on the northern elevation suggest the location of a former structure, possibly a timber-framed bakehouse.

The hall, which may have been timber-framed until this point, was probably rebuilt at much the same time. As rebuilt it exhibits a combination of large square dressed and smaller coarse dressed blocks. The window shows no evidence of having chamfered reveals or mullions.

The final significant phase in the house's development was the addition of a three storey brick structure to the front of the west cross-wing. The front elevation of the stone building was retained as an internal wall. The brick structure overlaps and abuts the west elevation of the stone structure, but is tied into the stone coursing of the hall. The rear elevations were not fenestrated. The west elevation and the new brick front were given the same windows. The upper windows in the north and east elevations of the east stone cross-wing were blocked and the door may have been inserted at that time.

The final phase dates to the early 19th century and probably coincides with the construction of Whiston Eaves Hall and stables, the latter having a

WHISTON EAVES FARM
BUILDINGS TAKEN
FROM THE WBB
MINERALS' REPORT.

date stone of 1808. This would suggest that the focus of the estate moved away from the farmstead which became occupied by a manager or tenant.

The other farm buildings
The north and east ranges are of early C20th date. The brick extension to the rear of the west range dates from between 1888 and 1900 and is a truncated part of an earlier stone building. The original west range was of four bays with entrances apparently to the west. The facade facing the courtyard would appear to have been rebuilt to allow the reordering of the interior and the insertion of a hay loft or granary. The range was further extended by the addition of a milk parlour to the north. In the early to mid 20th century, the roof of the whole range has been raised onto brick pillars and the roof and interior re-ordered into five bays. The external stone stairs abutting the range give access to the upper storey. Interesting architectural features include the remnants of a dove loft....

The stable block is listed grade II and apparently constructed in a single phase. A date stone above the gabled entrance on the courtyard side is of 1808. The gabled entrance provided the only access into the courtyard. A window to the north side of the entrance, with evidence of a lamp bracket over, suggests the employment of a gatekeeper.

Of the Hall itself we have no adequate description although the picture is well-known to the people of Whiston. The appearance points to construction during the early part of the 19th century which coincides with the assumption in the documents provided by WBB. The Smith family, who almost certainly had the hall built, were minor gentry of yeoman stock who had interests in business as well as farming. A reference to the Smith's involvement in tin coating can be found in the chapter on Oakamoor.

The other farm to suffer from the demand for aggregates and sand was Crowtrees, tenanted by the Harrisons, an old Whiston family. The family must have breathed a sigh of relief when the quarrying operation finally ended 'blasting' at the end of the 20th century. Now Chris Bickle and his wife, Diane (Harrison) have moved into the tourist trade, their bed and breakfast offering visitors to Alton Towers a taste of country living. The original farmhouse is one of the few reminders of life in the area before the sand quarrying.

British Industrial Sand eventually changed its name to Hepworth Minerals who later merged with WBB Ltd of Devon. WBB Minerals are engaged in plans to take down the old stable block in 2005 and utilise the stone by encouraging its use in local building projects.

WHISTON COPPER WORKS

The smelting works was built at the behest of the Duke of Devonshire and was fed almost exclusively by the ore produced from their mines at Ecton. Copper ore had been mined for centuries at Ecton and antler bone tools found in one section of the mine suggest that even Neolithic man may have engaged in extracting ore.

For centuries the mines operated spasmodically, the Devonshires choosing to lease the mines to others rather than be involved themselves. Dr Robert Plot, visiting the area in about 1686 commented:

..... *'the copper ore of the county must be referred to hither, not only as they are stones, but also as they include much sulphur, whereof there has been dug divers sorts out of Ecton Hill in the parish of Wetton, belonging to the right Honourable William, Earl of Devon. The mine was worked several years ago by my Lord of Devon himself, Sir Richard Fleetwood, and some Dutch men, but they had all left it off before I came to the country as not worth their while, copper coming cheaper from Sweden than they could make it here.'*

Plot further states: *'rock broken by gunpowder and produced 3 sorts of ore. 1 a black sort which was the best, 2 a yellow sort, the worst and 3, a mix of both. Smelted at Ellastone, not far off where they had mills.'*

The Devonshires proved to be shrewd business men. It suited their purposes to continue the policy of granting leases on the mine whilst retaining ownership until the true value of the mine was seen in 1723 when eight large deposits of copper ore were discovered. Between 1739 and 1760, the Devonshires became more and more aware of the success of the mines and a request to extend the lease after 1760 was turned down. The 5th Duke himself decided to operate the mine.

The mines produced more and more ore and ever greater profits. The revenue was vast and increased the fortunes of the Cavendish family. Between 1761 and 1775 a profit in excess of £78,000 was made from the sale of copper ore plus a small amount of lead. By 1790, over a twenty-eight year period, the mine produced a profit of £290,000.

The success of the Ecton mines soon outstripped the capacity of the smelting mills at Ellastone. Why the mill was not expanded is not clear. There were other outlets for the ore and other smelting facilities but the Duke had other plans. He opted to build a new smelting works at Whiston which would be large enough to handle the volume of ore coming out of Ecton. Why he chose Whiston is open to conjecture but it was close to the fuel from the Duke's own coalmines at Foxtwood and Hazles Cross. The Caldon canal was not in existence yet - the first reference to it, to facilitate the removal of limestone from Cauldon, did not occur until 1775 and it was in use in 1778. Perhaps the Duke felt sure of its construction when he planned the smelter? As an astute businessman of high social standing, the Duke would have been only too aware of the opportunities offered by the canal system. The fact that in later years a railway was laid only a few yards away from the smelting works was even more fortuitous.

The land at Whiston was purchased for the sum of £250, a considerable sum, and local roads would have had to be improved to cope with traffic. The Whiston smelter was constructed in 1770 adjacent to a road now referred to as Black Lane. On the site itself, eight furnaces were built, six for reducing the ore and two for refining. Five furnaces would have been in use at any one time, whilst the sixth was being rebuilt.

The smelter offered an alternative to the local agricultural workforce. Initially 23 men were employed: twelve smelters, four labourers and seven carriers, but the new venture was a huge success and by 1780 the quantity of ore coming out of Ecton had increased four fold. Staffing levels rose to sixty. The capacity of the Ecton mines remained at a peak for another decade, and it was not until 1798 that any decline was perceived.

WHISTON COPPER WORKS

Despite the reduction in capacity at Ecton and the corresponding reduction at Whiston, no attempt to obtain ore elsewhere appears to have been made. The smelter went into a steady decline and finally closed in 1818. But as luck would have it, others had their sights on the Whiston works. In 1821 it was sold to William Sneyd, Clement Sneyd and Thomas Sneyd-Kynnersley. The Sneyds were one of Staffordshire's most influential families. They saw the opportunity to process the ore produced by their own copper mines at Mixon. In 1828 a fourth partner was added, James Keys who owned the Cheadle Brass Works. For a sum of £437 he joined the Sneyds in a twenty-one year partnership and became the manager of the works now called William Sneyd & Co. at a salary of £2 a week plus a share of the profits.

The partnership was dissolved in March 1847 and the works sold to Keys for £3300. James Keys and his son John continued to trade here for many years. Much of the work came from the ore produced by small Staffordshire mines and a small amount from Ecton, but by 1890 even these were becoming depleted and the Whiston works closed its doors for the last time. The main works were demolished early in the 20th century and much of the stone used to build the new church. A few cottages remain as a reminder of what was once a thriving industry, the slag blocks defying all attempts at disguise by modernisation.

PROSPERITY IN THE VILLAGE

Along with the Copper Works came public houses, non-conformist chapels, schools, village shops and associated trades. The Ship Inn stood on Black Lane, close to the factory. It was closed in the 1960s and converted into a private house. Also converted into a private dwelling was the village store on Black Lane. More recently closed was the store and post office on the Whiston Eaves road. Of the other two pubs, only the Sneyd Arms remains. The Horse Shoe Inn, like the Ship, suffered when the copper works closed. The Sneyd Arms has recently followed the route of so many other village pubs and re-emerged as a restaurant and modernisation has removed all trace of the Blacksmith's forge that stood adjacent to the pub on the side of the Froghall road.

If Burtonwood ale slaked the thirst of the worker, then Methodism fed the soul. It swept like wildfire across the Staffordshire moorlands in the 19th century and nowhere was too remote or small for a meeting house or chapel. Froghall had its own chapel on the side of the Whiston road opposite Thomas Bolton's. In Whiston both Primitive and Wesleyan chapels were built in 1836. Earlier meetings were held in a cottage in the village. The Tunstall Primitive Methodist Circuit plan of 1812 refers to such a meeting place in Whiston.

The Primitive Methodists built a new chapel in 1907/8 and moved out of the original which was then converted into the house. Beneath the original chapel was a large cellar that was used as a Sunday school and may even have been a village day school - village children were certainly being taught there during the period when the village school was being built. A report in the *Cheadle and Tean Times & Advertiser* in 1910 also referred to a '*Lantern*

Lecture to be given in the school room of the Primitive Methodist School'. The Wesleyan Chapel continued to hold services in the original building close to Sycamore Farm until 1933 when the churches merged and began to worship in the Primitive Methodist Chapel - the 'new' chapel, now almost a hundred years old and still in regular use.

In 1897 a new parish of Foxt-Whiston formed and the village church at Whiston, dedicated to St. Mildred, arrived a decade later. The desire for a church of their own gained impetus when the opportunity arose to purchase the stone from the copper works. A book compiled by the children of the village and edited by their teacher, Joan Morris, records that the villagers approached the owners of the defunct copper works with a request to purchase the stone at a reasonable price. They could only afford the sum of £57-10s. For this 500 tons of stone was removed, plus the stone from a local cottage, in a mammoth task where farmers provided horses and carts and the men of the village volunteered their spare time and holidays. An appeal now raised the money to start the job:

Accounts to December 31st 1909

Stone from old copper works. Exors of late Jas. Keys Esq.	£ 57-00-00.
Taking down arches and walling. Mr W. Alcock.	£ 18-00-00.
Architects fees on account.	£ 25-00-00.
Builder, Mr W. Alcock. Cheadle. On account.	£ 225-00-00
Church Building Society appeal	£ 1-14-00
TOTAL	£ 326-14-00
Balance in hand	£ 25-04-07
TOTAL	£351-18-07

The earlier references to a schoolroom in the Chapel indicate the spasmodic nature of education prior to the Education Act of 1903. Dame schools and Sunday schools mainly provided the education of village children.

There is a reference to a school at Whiston in a document relating to Hugh Sleigh of Leek, which states that a school was founded by deed dated 10th May 1871. The school familiar to the older people of Whiston is the village school that was built after the Act of 1903.

Correspondence (SRO) from Graham Balfour MA, the County Education Officer gives us an interesting insight into a village school of the time:

'....the authority, having expressed considerable forebearance, must press for improvement of the natural lighting of the main room by 31st August 1909. Otherwise the Local Education Authority will cease to maintain the school'.

New earth closets were provided in 1912 but their use caused great consternation when the provision of earth was in short supply.

Praise and criticism were available in equal measure. The inspector's report dated 10th April 1913 noted that *'Order is good, and the children are attentive and industrious'*. Handwriting was described as good, and composition, as showing distinct promise.

The number of pupils in 1921/1923 was eighty-two and the ages ranged from four to fifteen years. Class 1 had forty-two pupils, class 2 had nineteen pupils and class 3 had twenty-one. The infant class contained the four to seven years old, the middle class consisted of the eight to ten years old and the rest, the eleven to fifteen years old, were taught by the head teacher. George William Ellerton was assisted by Martha Alcock and Lucy Alcock.

The report criticises the general standards and also points to the inclusion of 10 retarded scholars. Maypole dancing and drawing are noted as the best features, whilst arithmetic and reading are described as fair. *'Composition exercises are well written but show an evenness of common-place expression'*.

Some years later, in March 1926, a more critical report followed the inspector's visit: *'A quite remote rural school in a fair state of efficiency... staff has changed completely in the past three years. The Head Teacher and an inexperienced uncertified assistant, teach 53 children, and an uncertified teacher who suffers from partial deafness, instructs 37 youngsters in a separate room.'*

Not one iota of sympathy is expressed for the headteacher, who was battling against the odds with 90 pupils and inexperienced staff. Frederick Stew who was appointed 1st April 1925 and his staff consisted of Margaret Helen Anderson, assistant teacher, and Jessie Smith, the inexperienced teacher. Mr Stew demonstrated the character expected of a man in his position and he ensured that Margaret and Jessie made the grade - the three of them went on to regain the confidence of the inspector.

A headteacher could expect to earn around £380 per annum then and class teachers around £180 per annum. The school cleaner was paid around £20 per annum and a clerk might expect to earn around £80 per annum. The head teacher usually lived in the schoolhouse attached to the school.

The school and the schoolhouse were in a poor state of repair and the idea of a new school was gathering momentum. The cost of repairs and refurbishment were prohibitive, and the need for larger premises with more classrooms and more teachers was becoming evident.

The Local Education Authority had other ideas - the school's status was changed and Whiston Primary School emerged with fewer pupils. With the older pupils now attending local secondary schools, the size of the school was no longer considered a problem and the next decision to sell the schoolhouse met with little opposition. A report by Messrs. Fox and Harrison valued the

St Mildred's church, Whiston.

Whiston Hall.

house at £250. It was advertised locally in the *Cheadle Post & Times* as '*a semi-detached freehold dwelling house. Formerly the School House, Whiston Church of England School.*" It sold for about £700.

The sale of the house and the anticipated demise of the school itself, prompted the local community to seek first refusal for a village hall. The plea met with no success, but the villagers were not deterred from their objective and a fine, purpose-built village hall now stands on the side of the Whiston Eaves road. The school has continued as a primary school until 2005.

Whites Directory of 1834 describes Whiston as *a scattered village, four miles north-east of Cheadle*, and goes on.....

In this township are a few pits of small parts of small coal, the large brass and copper works of Wm. Sneyd & Co.

Whiston Eaves, a hamlet half a mile south. Froghall, one mile east of Whiston at the junction of the Caldon and Uttoxeter canals, where there is a large wharf, and a railway from the limestone quarries at Caldon Lowe. At Froghall there is also a paint and colour manufactory, and a corn mill, but the latter is in Ipstones parish. Mr Thomas Smith is the largest landowner and Lord of the Manor.

Residents

Philip Ball. Paint and Colour Manufacturer. Froghall House.

Thomas Cooper. Joiner.   Harvey Thomas. Butcher & Vict

Benjamin Keys. Manager. Lees   Jas Keys Copper Manufacture.

John Lane. Vict.   Hanh Pattinson. Wheelwright. Samuel Pattinson. Brickmaker.

Thomas Smith. Gentleman, Whiston Eaves.   Thomas Smith. Agent. Garston.

William Sneyd. Copper and Brass Manufacturer.

Trent and Mersey Canal Co. Limestone Merchants. Froghall wharf.

William Butler, Agent.   Charles Weston. Agent.

In the 1851 Whites Directory the names are beginning to change. The canal to Uttoxeter has been partly filled up and converted to a railway:

Residents.

Thomas Alcock. Shop-Keeper. Vict.   P. Ball. Paint Manufacturer. Froghall.

James Beardmore. Vict; and Smith. Horse Shoe Inn.

Joseph Cooper. Joiner.   Charles Eaton. Taylor.

Josiah Fernihough. Timber Merchant and Vict; Navigation Arms.

William Gaunt. Agent. Froghall.

Joseph Harvey. Butcher and Vict; Nelson. Oakamoor.

Horatio Hifford. Station Master. Froghall.   Charles Kent. Shoemaker.

Jas. Keys. Brass and Copper Manufacturer.

N.S. Railway Co. Lime Merchants.

Thomas Smith. Gentleman. Whiston Grange.

Shopkeepers: J. Fernihough, Wm. Hughes, Thomas Kent (shoemaker), John Mosley.

Directories listed the names of prominent citizens - the people on whom the village depended. Philip Ball lived at Froghall House and probably employed a manager who lived on the factory premises. Thomas Cooper and Joseph Cooper were ancestors of the Coopers who inherited the Whiston Hall estate. The Keys, of Germanic origin, were the original builders and occupiers of Whiston Hall and for a few decades one of the most influential family in the village. The brickmaker, Samuel Pattinson, may have worked at the brickworks in Froghall although bricks and tiles may also have been made in Whiston.

A winding mechanism of one of the cableways that brought the limestone down through Whiston to Froghall from Cauldon Lowe. There were manually-operated breaking points along the course of the track, including in Whiston.

It is also interesting to note James Beardmore - the Horse Shoe Inn took its name from the other occupation of the landlord who was a blacksmith. Joseph Fernihough, timber merchant and victualler of the Navigation Arms, no doubt, lived close to the Caldon canal. The term navigator was in common use and relates to the 'navvies' who dug the waterways.

WHISTON HALL

Millicent Forrester was a young chambermaid employed by the Keys at Whiston Hall and she fell for the charms of the master, John Keys, and bore him two children. John brought them up as part of his family and both took the name Keys. From the gravestone in the churchyard of St. Giles the Abbot, Cheadle, we have these records.

James Keys of Whiston   Died 12th June 1854 Age 69.
Margaret Rehuit of the above name.
James Keys Whiston   Died 1st September 1870 Age 78.
James Keys   Died 24th February 1907 Age 45.

When John died, the contents of his will caused quite a stir. He left everything to Millicent. The chambermaid found herself the owner of several farms, a quarry, various cottages and Whiston Hall. In the course of time, she married a Mr Cooper, probably Joseph, and had another child, Thomas.

Thomas inherited the estate when Millicent died about 1960 and he made the transfer easily enough from the traditional family occupation of joinery, to farmer and estate owner. He was a well-known figure in the village, happy to work on the land and enter into whatever entrepreneurial scheme took his fancy. His business interests were the quarrying of silica sand and the pursuit of golf.

Thomas started the Whiston Hall Golf Club in the 1960s, initially for his own pleasure and that of his friends. It quickly became evident that the golf course would prove very popular and it gradually evolved into a financially viable business. Membership fees were modest and there was a constant demand from people keen to enter the world of golf. With the facilities within the Hall, the splendid views, a lack of pretension and the expansion to eighteen holes, the Whiston Golf Club quickly became a valued part of the Cooper estate.

In almost a repeat of history, when Thomas died in 1992, he by-passed his immediate family and left the estate in its entirety to his grand-daughter, Louise. Louise, just eighteen at the time, had not seen her grandfather for several years. Family discussions and legal redress were sought. A redistribution of the will was proposed and went ahead and all seemed well again.

But not for long! As Louise grew older and wiser, she began to ponder what might have been. Thomas's immediate family were of the opinion that they had done the right thing but Louise asked for the case to be reviewed, and once again the Whiston Estate was on public view. Finally the case reached the High Court - and the matter was settled on the steps of the court. The farms and the Sneyd Arms public house would remain in the hands of Thomas's immediate family. Whiston Hall Farm and the Golf Course would belong to Louise.

A DASTARDLY DEED

This peaceful village was once home to a dastardly crime, a murder that involved the death of Tom Smith, a member of the local gentry who lived at Whiston Eaves Hall.

Adjacent to Whiston Eaves stands the hamlet of Moneystone, much of its lands now obliterated by quarrying, but in 1866 open farmland in the control of the Smith family. It was the custom of local people to engage in a little poaching and although it was tolerated by the Smiths, it was a thorn in their sides. The annoyance was exacerbated by William Collier, who lived at Oldfields Farm. A farm was perhaps too generous a description for 36 acres,

barely enough to
sustain Collier and
his family. Poaching
was almost essential
and the relationship
between Collier and
Smith was not eased
by the intransigence
of Collier over a
dispute concerning a
water course.

The poaching,
hitherto an annoyance,
now became a major
issue and Thomas

Whiston Eaves Hall.

Smith, the eldest son and heir to the family fortune, determined to catch Collier
in the act. In 1866, crimes such as poaching and sheep stealing were serious
indeed and by catching Collier, the Smiths would have had little trouble in
removing him from the farm - and the area.

On the night of July 5th 1866, Thomas Smith and one of the farm hands
named Bamford, retired early with the intention of rising early to catch Collier
red-handed. As often happens, the course of events now took an unexpected
turn. Smith arose before Bamford and without waiting for him set off towards
the plantations where their game birds were kept. Collier was heading in the
same direction and the two of them met on the edge of Barn Plantation.

A bitter row ensued, during which Collier lost his temper and flew into a
violent rage. Smith decided upon a hasty retreat but as he turned to run, Collier
raised his gun, took aim and fired. The shot caught Smith on the back of the
head, blasting away his hat and leaving him seriously wounded. Collier now set
about Smith, striking him about the head with his gun, before leaving him on
the ground as he fled the scene, pausing only to hide his gun in a land drain on
the edge of one of his fields.

The crime was discovered the following morning when the Smiths,
concerned at Tom's absence at breakfast, organised a search party.

Tongues began to wag, and Collier became the subject of gossip. People
spoke of gunshots in the night, and of Collier's dispute with the Smiths.
Retribution was swift in those days. The police had a body and a suspect. All
they needed was 'evidence' and, that came readily enough, although today it
would be laughed out of court. Their first witness was Eliza Taylor of

Moneystone. Eliza stated that she heard two gunshots at 3.00am. A common enough occurrence during the poaching season! Another witness, Henry Goldstraw, also claimed to have heard two shots at around 3.30am.

More damaging was the evidence of Eliza Moorcroft. On what was noted to be a bright, moonlight night, Eliza claimed to have seen Collier walking in the vicinity of the Garston Road, heading towards the culverts on the edge of his fields. The following morning, Eliza's husband had conducted a search of Collier's fields and discovered the stock and barrel of a gun, pushed at arm's length up a draining culvert. It was enough to arrest William Collier and, in the course of events, to see him hanged for the murder of Thomas Smith.

The initial reaction of the trial judge was to record his disquiet at the evidence. The jury, at one point, also found the evidence unsatisfactory and asked for guidance. Notwithstanding this, William Collier, was found guilty and sentenced to be hanged outside Stafford Gaol on Tuesday 7th August 1866. It may have come as a relief to some when Collier confessed to his crime a few days before his execution.

On the day of the execution, a crowd of 2,000 onlookers crammed into Gaol Square to witness the hanging, but the execution did not go to plan. As the trapdoor opened, Collier fell to the ground as the rope failed. Collier lay there, shaking and bruised, as the executioner helped him to his feet. The stunned crowd found their voice and yelled out cries of *'freedom'* and *'liberty'* but the emotion had little effect on the officials and Collier was prepared, once again. This time no mistake was made and William paid the ultimate price.

Whether the unfortunate incident influenced the authorities or whether the vociferous reaction of the crowd played a part is not clear, but William Collier was the last person to be executed in public outside Stafford Gaol.

EXECUTION OF WILLIAM COLLIER

At Stafford, on Tuesday, August 7, 1866, for the Murder of Thomas Smith, jun., of Whiston Eaves, near Cheadle.

Staffordshire Summer Assizes.

Before Mr. JUSTICE SHEE.

The Murder at Whiston Eaves.

WILLIAM COLLIER, farmer, was indicted for the wilful murder of Thomas Smith, the younger, on the 5th July, 1866, at Whiston Eaves parish of Kingsley. The following are the leading facts of the case, as proved by the witnesses called:—

Mr. Smith was the eldest son of Mr. Thomas Smith, a gentleman well known in Cheadle and the neighbourhood. He is lord of the manor of Whiston, and is also a farmer on a considerable scale. Deceased was his eldest son, and about 24 years of age. He was an active, frank, agreeable young gent eman, and popular with all classes in the neighbourhood, and was familiarly

Governor in the customary form to deliver up the body of the culprit for public execution.

The culprit was taken into the corridor of the new prison, where the officers of justice and the Rev. M O'Sullivan with the last executioner of the law, Smith, the hangsman awaited his arrival. After a deliberate arrangement of all the sad details of the execution, the procession started for the place of execution.

The procession having arrived at the lodge, the culprit was taken into the Governor's office and underwent the process of pinioning, in the presence of the officials.

Oakamoor Weir - a weir of course usually indicating a mill.

The Station — Oakamoor

Chapter Seven
Oakamoor

CHEADLE

Strictly speaking, Cheadle lies beyond the confines of the Churnet Valley but it would be impossible to overlook this close neighbour of Oakamoor and Alton whose history is so interconnected with both them and the Churnet. Cheadle was a prosperous little town, with an ancient weekly market.

The Cheadle coalfields provided much of the energy that later on powered the mills and factories of the Churnet Valley and they were responsible for the decision of Thomas Patten to build the Cheadle Brass Company. Patten had great influence in the area, both socially and industrially. Equally important was Cheadle Mill, an extension of the prosperous textile business of J.N. Phillips of Tean. The Tape Street mill, originated in the 1790s and extended in 1823, is a substantial building which provided much employment for almost 200 years.

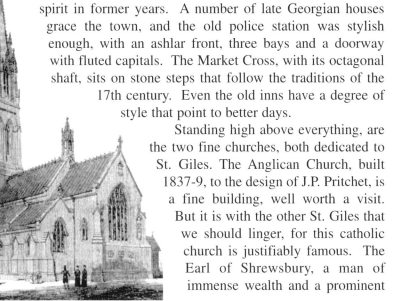

A host of smaller businesses and a thriving high street gave Cheadle an air of prosperity that has been eroded in the 20th century. To the outsider, Cheadle would now benefit greatly from regeneration. It was certainly not lacking in style or spirit in former years. A number of late Georgian houses grace the town, and the old police station was stylish enough, with an ashlar front, three bays and a doorway with fluted capitals. The Market Cross, with its octagonal shaft, sits on stone steps that follow the traditions of the 17th century. Even the old inns have a degree of style that point to better days.

Standing high above everything, are the two fine churches, both dedicated to St. Giles. The Anglican Church, built 1837-9, to the design of J.P. Pritchet, is a fine building, well worth a visit. But it is with the other St. Giles that we should linger, for this catholic church is justifiably famous. The Earl of Shrewsbury, a man of immense wealth and a prominent catholic, financed the building of the church in 1841-46 and engaged A.W.N. Pugin to design what was to become a masterpiece. Considered by some to be Pugin's greatest work, the Neo-gothic St. Giles stands as a monument of Victorian splendour.

The steeple dominates, of course, but from all angles, Pugin's decorative style attracts the eye. The east window has five lights, with the four petal motif at the top. In the chancel are sedilia and piscina, opposite the Easter Sepulchre recess. The south porch has a pointed tunnel vault with transverse arches. Paint work and decorative floor tiles give a feeling of freedom that Pugin must have relished. Even the font, the reredos and the pulpit bear the influence of Pugin, whilst outside the church he provided inspiration for the high crocketed cross that stands in the graveyard.

Pugin also stamped his mark on the surrounding buildings, as if to make sure that his masterpiece would not be blemished by unsightly neighbours. The school is of brick and combines the Pugin asymmetrical front with a utilitarian back wing complete with buttresses and regular fenestration. To the south is the Convent of St. Joseph with tower, saddleback roof and a little wooden cloister.

Pugin's church remains as impressive now as it was when Nikolaus Pevsner described it so vividly in his *Buildings of England* series.

CHEADLE BRASS COMPANY

Sometimes referred to as the Cheadle Brass & Copper Company, this business was established at the Spout, near Brookhouse, Cheadle, in 1734. The proprietor, Thomas Patten, employed a local man, Robert Hurst, as a partner. Hurst had knowledge of the Alton area which would have been useful to Patten when he established a brass wire mill there in the same year.

Patten inherited his business acumen and wealth from his father, Thomas Patten senior, a trader who worked on the Mersey and was involved in making the river navigable for shipping from Runcorn to Warrington in the 1690s. Thomas junior, 1690-1772 was born at the beginning of his father's power. The opening of the Mersey to shipping encouraged his building of the first copper smelting works in Lancashire on Bank Quay in Warrington in 1719. When he died in 1726, Thomas junior inherited the family business.

Thomas's first move was to set up a brass works and a brass wire works to take advantage of the copper being produced at Warrington. With considerable foresight, Thomas set up his business with Birmingham and the Black Country, the emerging industrial capital of England, in mind. Cheadle also offered another vital ingredient - the Cheadle coalfields were extensive and of good quality. Transportation of coal, a major expense, would be virtually eliminated.

The Churnet Valley offered tradesmen skilled in the metalworking. Even so, in the initial stages, Patten employed experienced brass smelters from Germany and Holland. Among the German contingent was John Essor, to whom Patten paid ten guineas for travelling expenses. Essor settled in quickly and decided to stay. After a time he changed his name to Keys and he and his family became the chief smelters in the Patten factories.

Thomas Patten ran an efficient and profitable business, and the family thrived. For many years the Cheadle Brass Company was considered to be the leader in the field of brass technology. The Patten empire grew. With an eye on the expanding slave trade, he acquired, in 1743, a site near Holywell in North Wales where a copper mill was built to make Guinea rods for the African trade. Cheadle gained extra trade when the Warrington factory was leased out and the copper smelting was transferred to Cheadle, and in 1768 a new copper smelting works was built close to Woodhead colliery to cope with the volume of ore being produced by the Duke of Devonshire's mines at Ecton. Further consolidation in 1788 in the Cheadle and Alton works plus the purchase of a tin plate works at Oakamoor in 1790, ensured Patten's continued prosperity.

But now the zinc spelter method of brass production was proving popular and with set up costs substantially lower than traditional machinery the brass users in Birmingham were suddenly keen to make their own brass. Whether the Patten family thought they were invincible, a degree of complacency set in. Their children were now educated in the classics, and politics superseded trade. The changes may not have been apparent in the 1790s when the company stocks were valued at £60,000, even less during the inflation that accompanied the Napoleonic war, but it soon was during the recession that followed.

The company was forced to retrench. In 1821 salaries were cut. The works manager, William Keates, was sent to Neath Abbey to close down the works. The closing of the Cheadle works was considered but they struggled on for a while until, in 1828, the Alton wire mill was closed and production transferred to a newer wire mill at Oakamoor. The manager at Alton, John Brindley, a relative of the canal engineer, attempted to keep the mills running himself but was unsuccessful and went into liquidation in 1834. The era of wire making at Alton came to an end and the premises moved to paper-making.

The Cheadle works struggled on until the end of the 1830s when Patten leased the premises to James Keys, a descendant of the original expert, Essor, brought over from Germany. James and his son also managed the Whiston Copper Works and eventually purchased both factories, Whiston in 1847 for £3,300 and Cheadle in 1856 for £2,150.

The remnants of the Patten empire survived at Oakamoor. Production figures for 1844 reveal a total of 380 tons of copper. By 1848 it had fallen to 288 tons, 1849 to 214 tons, 1850 just 127 tons and only 20 tons in 1851. The company closed and the Patten dynasty was confined to history.

When the Oakamoor and Cheadle works were put up for sale by auction, no acceptable bid was received. Thomas Bolton of Birmingham were approached and they confirmed their interest. Thomas saw the potential in copper telegraph wire and with his son, Alfred, visited the Oakamoor site on 18th February 1852, along with Francis Edwards and Charles Wollaston, directors of the Channel Submarine Telegraph Company. Bolton's were in dire need of space. Expansion at their Broad Street premises in Birmingham was virtually impossible and Oakamoor offered a large and spacious opportunity.

Thomas timed his bid to perfection. The Oakamoor works had again been offered for sale in the Mining Journal of 1852 with an auction date fixed for March 2nd to 4th. Alfred Bolton met the Patten lawyers on February 23rd and made them an offer of £7,750 for the Oakamoor works, including its stock, machinery, cottages and property. The offer was accepted the following day. The agreement was formalised on 1st March when the sale agreement was signed by Thomas Bolton and J.W. Patten. A further £5,000 changed hands on 1st May when Thomas purchased the freehold.

The purchase of the copper works and its appendages had cost a total of £12,750. Even allowing for the financial differences of the time, the sum represents a remarkable and shrewd decision. Alfred Bolton was about to transform the copper industry - as we have seen in the Froghall chapter.

ANCIENT OAKAMOOR

Oke appears in the records, as does Okemoor and Oakwallmoor. Like most of the hamlets in the Churnet Valley, Oakamoor was important through the part it played in the extraction of iron ore and the forging of wrought iron. Unlike many of the other hamlets and villages Oakamoor was not significant enough to merit inclusion in the Domesday survey. It also seems to have escaped the attention of the Saxon Chronicles.

Oke, or Okemoor was a part of the waste-lands within the boundary of the Totmanslow hundred. The definition of waste-land was, *'uncultivated, sparsely populated, desolate, unused and unproductive'*. The description would suffice whether the area was moorland or woodland, in the case of Oakamoor, woodland. The use of waste-land, and the timber within it, is recorded in detail by the monks of Croxden abbey.

Elsewhere in this book we have reason to be grateful for the scholarship of those ancient scribes. For our purposes, the entries that relate to the Churnet

Valley are clear enough. The Abbey was founded in 1179-1180 by the Verduns of Alveston (Alton) during the time of Bertram de Verdun (1140-1192). It is recorded that Bertram gave land at Chotes to found an abbey. Chotes, in turn became Chotene and, in modern parlance, Cotton. Unfortunately the name Cotton is not uncommon in the area and proof positive that the land referred to is the Cotton near to Oakamoor is lacking.

Not that it alters our story, for within a short period of time the land was rejected for a more fertile area near to Hollington. The picturesque valley extended to the banks of the Churnet and the Dove and bore the splendid name of St. Mary's Vale. Here the Cistercian monks dedicated their labours and their piety to St. Mary. The records maintained by the monks illustrate not only the business activities of the abbey but also the major events that affected their lives. What will the proponents of global warming make of the following:

1290 Wood called Gibbe Ruydinges was burnt (The woodlands were used by charcoal burners on a regular basis and this particular wood in Oakamoor provided a useful income for the abbey).

1297 The Church at Leek was burnt down together with the whole town, by mischance.

1299. On the day of S.S.Fabian and Sebastian a violent storm blew up from the south and blew down a wall near Lehee for 60ft in length and in a garden adjoining tore up by the roots and broke into pieces forty great apple trees and a very large pear tree and the wind prevailed though not with the same violence for a month or more.

1301. Great earthquake took place.

1319. A plague or murrain of animals unseen and unheard of hitherto raged through the whole country. Innumerable thousands of bulls, cows, yearlings and calves were killed suddenly and with an acute fever. Croxden sustained losses amounting to 200 marks.

1329. The under wood of the park of Oke was sold to William Carpenter and Thomas Le Boys in gross for £24.

1361. A pestilence in which every child born since the first plague died. (A whole generation lost. Details relating to the Black Death in the Oakamoor area or the Churnet valley are not readily available. It is indicative of the lethal nature of the plague that it should reach even the remote areas of the country. By 1361, iron working was already in progress and contact with outside sources would assist the spread of this awful disease)

1372. And a house in the grange of Oke, near the road was built anew and enlarged 'unam finem' beyond the former grange. In the same year was a great flood on the 20th August so that all the grass and corn growing near the water was destroyed and all the bridges standing over the Chyrnet were totally destroyed.

At the end of the 13th century the abbey had six granges within the immediate vicinity, Croxden, Cheadle, Musden, Oke, Crakemarsh and Caldon. They also had land outside the area at Oaken, part of the parish of Codsall, near Wolverhampton, where they also had a Grange. The size of the abbey necessitated the employment of local people to work the land. It also attracted individuals who sought to follow a life of devotion. Their names indicate their origins. The earliest recorded is Richard de Ipstones. Also recorded are:

> Geoffrey de Farley.
> Thomas de Roucester.
> William of Uttokishather.
> Ralph de Crakemarsh.
> John de Uttockeshather.
> Henry de Denstone.
> Thomas de Farley.
> John de Uttokesherter.

With the dissolution of the monastery in 1538 the records of Croxden Abbey passed to Sir Walter Leveson (now part of the Sutherland Collection).

INDUSTRY IN THE VALLEY
Industry in the valley now continued at a pace. The assize records and the Shrewsbury Rentals were studied at length by Herbert Chester for his research on the Churnet valley. We learn the following about an Assize Case concerning the forge at Oakamoor:

2nd May. 1573. Forge Okam More in Alveston.
Ralph Lee of Alverton, yeoman, alleges that George, Earl of Shrewsbury, was seized of a messuage and lands near Greendale called Oakam More upon which lands was built a forge or iron works with other necessary houses, barns and buildings. He demised these premises for a term of years to one Nicholas Lycette who about a year ago granted his interest in them to Ralph Lee of Alverton, Yeoman who accordingly entered into and enjoyed them until Nicholas Wooley of Orton (Alton) and Henry Copestake of Farley Yeomen claimed two barns'.

So we are made aware of a forge at Oakamoor in 1573 and it may well be that the same site was used for successive forging operations over previous centuries. There would also be little point in building elsewhere if an already successful works was available. Without being credited to record, the site appears to have been known locally as Caldwall. Adjacent stood the smithy referred to in the Victorian County History as Hungerwall (1539).

It appears that the forge passed from the ownership of the Queen in 1564 when it was purchased by Thomas Westwood. Westwood sold it to Symon Herring and in 1647 Agnes Herring sold it to Thomas Jenkinson. From Jenkinson the business passed to Joseph Bristow. Bristow and Jenkinson were ironmasters and were, no doubt, attracted to a recently restored forge operating in the midst of a readily available supply of iron ore.

The leading ironmaster in Staffordshire at the time was Richard Foley. In 1663, Foley leased the Meir Heath furnace from Sir John Bill of Morton. The Meir Heath furnace had begun life a few years after the 'Old Furnace' had ceased production and, like it, depended on the output of ore from the Churnet valley. Foley became the dominant force in what became known as the Staffordshire Partnership. Foley acquired possession of the forge and hammer mills at Oakamoor and at Consall, gaining control of iron in the valley.

The Partnership enlarged the Oakamoor forge and mills and developed a large pool to the north of the site. The Churnet had been subjected to numerous changes over the years and the construction of weirs, pools and mill-races was par for course. How much these changes were responsible for the flooding, which was an annual event, is difficult to say but, until relatively recent times, the river ran anywhere but along its original course. The wooden bridges that spanned the Churnet between Leek and Rocester were frequently washed away during winter rains and it was not until stone bridges were built in the 17th century that access to villages was guaranteed.

The Oakamoor works is referred to by Foley as Oakwallmoor Forge. The business remained with the family for many years. Richard died in 1678 and the business passed to his son, also Richard. The second Richard died in 1682 and the business passed to an uncle, John Foley, who died in 1685. John appears to be the Foley referred to by Herbert Chester, who credits him as living at Longton Hall. From John it passed to his brother-in-law, Henry Glover who became a major shareholder in both the Oakamoor and Consall works.

On Glover's demise the business passed briefly to John Wheeler and then to their manager, Obidiah Lane who became managing director. He employed two managing secretaries, Richard Locker at the Consall works and Robert Hurst at Oakamoor. The name Hurst is of significance - the name occurs in 1734 when another Hurst is employed by Thomas Patten as a junior partner. The Hursts seem to have held important positions in the Oakamoor iron trade for several decades.

Tin-coating was well established by 1761 when the works was visited by a Swedish industrialist, Johan Ludvig Robsaham. At the time the owner and director of the Oakamoor works was George Kendall. Kendall was involved with the Oakamoor works for around twenty-one years and his contribution was unique. He introduced tin plating to Oakamoor and in doing so extended the life of the mill. Robsaham's report, which was extremely positive, noted that both of the 1694 forge buildings were still in use, the old forge continued to refine and make bar and plate and at a second forge, the Tin Mill, the tinning application took place.

The Oakamoor site thrived and provided a prosperous living for Kendall. He settled down in the village and purchased the land from Stoneygate to the present railway tunnel, including Longhursts, Moss's Bank, the Pringle and the woodland which included Moss's Tenement. The mansion Kendall had built was later called The Lodge when it became the home of Dr Bearblock, a director and family member of the Thomas Bolton Copper Works.

The business now passed to George Smith and Henry Knifton, described in the Bailey Directory of 1784 as Tin Merchants. Smith was a member of the prosperous local gentry and lived at Whiston Eaves Hall. Knifton was from Alton, where his family had been grocers for many years. Knifton appears to have struggled to meet his financial arrangements although he still managed to purchase a property on the Farley side of the valley which later became known as Knifton's Tenement.

The new owners attempted other ventures. Nail-making looked promising for a while and a reference is found to *'a plot of land on which a new nail shop lately stood'*. The reference is dated 1787.

In 1790, Foley received an approach from Thomas Patten of the Cheadle Brass Co who offered to buy the Tin Plate Works outright. The sale was agreed and Smith and Knifton continued for a few more years with the lease transferred to Patten but by 1793 they had reached the end of their patience. Part of the works was already occupied for the production of copper under Robert Leigh. Although the iron trade took a few decades to finally leave the valley, the age of copper was about to arrive.

The Patten story at Oakamoor can be found on earlier pages. The decline of the Patten dynasty had already begun and the transition to copper reached a conclusion when they sold the Oakamoor site to the Bolton family.

There are two other ironworking sites known of at Oakamoor. At Eastwall farm, as noted earlier, evidence of a forge has long been apparent. The *Secunda Carta of Chedle* refers to *'the old mines of iron and my old forge, with two or three other amenities'*. The document is dated 1290 and is the earliest reference to iron working in the valley, The *'other amenities'* related to coal mines (Le Brode Delph). Significant quantities of hematite slag (waste) that originated in Consall found its way to Eastwall, indicating a trading relationship. Plateways exist around the Hawksmoor and Eastwall area although the form of transport was likely to have been by mule or perhaps the Churnet. As for the forge itself, an idea of the methods employed can be gained from the huge amounts of slag that surround the site. Much of the slag was subjected to reworking in later years, indicating that the heat of the furnace was only achieved by hand bellows. When the Old Furnace was built, around 1593, the extra heat generated enabled more iron to be extracted from the Eastwall slag.

The other site was at Old Furnace. The death of the Earl of Shrewsbury in 1590 created problems for tenants who had their premises on the Earl's land. Simon Herring was among those to be inconvenienced, as were his sub-tenants.

Coinciding with the Earl's death was the improved method of iron making which made the existing methods virtually redundant. The Earl's widow took advantage of the new methods and, after a period of quiet, Herring's forges and hammer mills, albeit much changed and extended, were once again contributing to local industry. The administration of the Earl's estate now fell to Bess of Hardwick. Bess, or the Countess Elizabeth, had become a very wealthy woman with an income almost as great as that of the Queen, Elizabeth I.

The Oakamoor estate may have seemed remote to Bess but she was shrewd enough to benefit from it. Others involved with the manufacture of iron were only too keen to take on Oakamoor and to pay for the privilege. Bess also received rent for the use of the water that powered the bellows and the forge.

Lawrence Loggin of Ashby de la Zouche was involved in building and running furnaces and forges. Loggin selected the site we now refer to as Old Furnace. The site was on the edge of Dimmingsdale on what was then the main road between Cheadle and Oakamoor was finally built and put into production in 1593. No trace of the furnace remains, although the footpath from Dimmingsdale passes close to its western extremes before beginning its return alongside a row of cottages that occupy the site. Across the road from the cottages the remains of the mill-pool can still be seen as can the mill race that passes under the road and alongside the cottages. The cottages themselves were built in the 19th century, the end one named Old Furnace being precisely dated as 1869. Evidence of an earlier building may be seen in the section of stone work incorporated into the central cottage. The area has numerous quarries but the stone in the cottage is almost certainly from Hollington.

The life of the furnace was relatively short and is thought to have closed in 1608 but the final chapter in the story of Eastwall and Old Furnace has still not been written. In the summer of 2003 the Time Team from Channel 4 visited the sites following an invitation from the owners of Old Furnace Cottage and under the guidance of Wessex Archaeology conducted a thorough investigation and a limited excavation. At Eastwall, examination of the slag vindicated the

Old Furnace.

Dimmingsdale Mill.

long held belief that a bloomery, operated by hand bellows, was used to produce iron. The site at Eastwall farm occupies the orchard and an adjacent field to the north east of the farm and the geophysical survey helped reveal a well-preserved base of a bloomery furnace dating from the 13th-14th century. Examination of the bloomery revealed the clay built furnace, the tapping arch and channel, the location of the bellows and some bloomery slag.

At the Old Furnace site it was thought that the furnace and a casting shop lay beneath the cottages. In the garden of the centre cottage a small pit was dug, measuring one metre square. A number of trenches were also dug in the garden and close to the stream. Altogether 300 pieces of pottery were found ranging from the 16th to the 18th and 19th centuries. More significantly, an unstratified sherd of late Saxon pottery was found at Old Furnace. This was examined by Debbie Ford of the Hanley Museum, who dated it to the 10/11th century. Perhaps the interim conclusion we can draw from this discovery is that the Old Furnace site is older than anticipated. Lawrence Loggin may not have built on a virgin site but on a site used by our Saxon forebears.

THOMAS BOLTON & SON LTD

When Bolton's purchased the Oakamoor works from Patten's Cheadle Brass & Copper Co in 1752 they came with a wealth of experience in the brass trade.

Samuel Bolton had established himself in the Black Country town of Walsall where he worked as a white-smith. Walsall had a reputation for the manufacture of saddles and harnesses and the trappings were made from brass. The cottage industries of the Midland towns were beginning to disappear and Birmingham grew quickly, from village to town, and finally to city with a large proportion of the population employed in the metal trade. Brass working, brass and copper alloys, iron working and associated trades made it the centre of industrial excellence.

Samuel moved into buckle making. When he died in 1781, his business passed to his son, Richard, who traded as Richard Bolton & Co of New Street, Walsall. By 1794 he was trading from a larger premises at 52 New Street, Birmingham where he concentrated more on being a metal merchant than a manufacturer. Richard died in 1812, a comparatively wealthy man and the business passed to Thomas. By 1820, at the age of thirty, he was in full charge and the company bore the title Thomas Bolton & Co.

In 1824, Thomas married Sarah Frances of Edgbaston. Thomas Bolton & Co had considerable trade with the USA and it was through the good intent of their Boston agent, William. D. Sohier that the first son of Thomas and Sarah was christened Alfred Sohier Bolton. A cup, suitably inscribed as being given *'by his father's esteemed friend'* was presented to Alfred in 1834. The cup is still in possession of the Bolton family. This connection with America no doubt proved a valuable asset in later years when sub-marine cable technology was in its infancy.

In the 1830s fortunes were being made by the manufacturers of copper and brass and by the rolling of brass plate. Thomas was determined to continue in manufacturing and by 1841 had sold his interest in the merchant house that had provided so well for his family. The Post Office Directory of 1845 refers to Thomas as a manufacturer of rolled metals, wires and tubes etc. When his son, Alfred eventually took over, the age of electricity was in its infancy. The Bolton's embraced the opportunity and were on a par with Crompton and Ferranti, the pioneers of electrical power.

By 1850, 2,215 miles of telegraph wire for communication had been erected in Britain. The English Channel Submarine Telegraph Company was developing their expertise in the use of marine cables. The shortcomings of standard copper wire for conduction were becoming apparent and the Bolton's spent time and money in improving the method of manufacturing. So successful did the company become that they established themselves as one of the most

The original brass and copper works at the turn of the 20th century.

competent wire makers in the world. The demand for their wire outgrew the capacity of the Broad Street works and expansion became essential.

The Oakamoor works offered Alfred the ideal solution - details are recorded in the Froghall chapter. The purchase was completed in 1852 and the men and women of Oakamoor were delighted. Now, instead of working in an ailing industry, they were employed by a dynamic, go ahead family at the forefront of modern technology.

A total of 239 tons of copper telegraph wire was produced in 1853. The first foreign order was from Denmark for a cable to cross the Denmark Strait. In 1854 another seven sub-marine cables were laid and the demand for Bolton's wire stretched the company to capacity. 1855 saw major expansion as the company prepared itself for even greater volume.

In 1856 The Atlantic Telegraph Company was formed by Cyrus Field, Charles Bright, John Brett and O.E. Whitehouse. Their object was to lay a cable between Europe and Newfoundland before 1862 and pioneer verbal communication between the continents. The importance of the venture encouraged the British Government to guarantee a return of £14,000 per annum when the line was working. A similar guarantee was received from the American Government. Bolton's were among the companies selected to supply the components; once again Oakamoor found itself working '*flat out*'.

A cable of such length had not been attempted before and problems occurred almost immediately. The cable was made in two halves with the intention of joining them in mid-Atlantic. Starting from Valentia Bay on the south coast of Ireland the British ship *Agamemnon* and the US ship *Niagara* laid 334 miles of cable before disaster struck. At a depth of 2,000 fathoms the cable broke and the expedition ground to a halt. Further trials and an insistence that high conductivity wire was used resulted in a second attempt in 1858. This time two ships started in mid Atlantic and, steaming in opposite directions, successfully laid the cable.

In America and Britain champagne corks popped at parties to celebrate the new era of communication, but the euphoria lasted only a few weeks. Faults developed and the signals became weak and fragmented. A total of seven hundred messages were sent before the line failed completely. But lessons had been learnt. It was obvious that far greater conductivity was required and Alfred Bolton made it his mission to bring about the necessary improvements. There can be no doubt that the work at Bolton's enabled submarine cable technology to advance at a pace. The Oakamoor works experimented with both solid copper and twisted strands before reaching a conductivity level of 96%.

Bolton's were involved in producing cables for all the leading telegraph companies, the Falmouth to Gibraltar cable was one of many. By 1863 they were once again ready to take on the Atlantic. A second attempt was proposed and a conductivity standard of 85% was specified. The wire was required in lengths of about a quarter of a mile. The 18 gauge wire was stranded into a conductor of seven wires weighing three hundred pounds per mile. Bolton's completed the work by 1865 and the laying of the cable began. Disaster struck again. The line broke and 1,186 miles of copper cable fell to the sea bed. Another cable was ordered immediately and Bolton's pulled out the stops again

Again the Great Eastern sailed with its valuable cargo and on July 27th 1866 the cable finally reached its destination. Alfred celebrated by buying himself a grand piano, and elsewhere wild parties greeted the success of the transatlantic telegraph. More good news followed. Attempts to recover the lost cable were successful and it was joined to the final length of cable to ensure a second line of communication across the Atlantic.

The success of the cables and the growing reputation of Bolton's telegraph wire brought in more and more orders, and when the submarine cable laying started to peak, they were able to make the switch to land telegraph wires and electricity wires. Alfred was not one to sit on his laurels. The production of tubes and rollers was also expanded, as was plate rolling.

Other factories were opened as the company sought new ventures. J.F. Allen of Widnes were bankrupt in 1881 and Alfred purchased the company that had specialised in copper refining. Years later, Bolton's became involved in the production of aluminium with a large factory in Milton, Stoke-on-Trent. Alfred's success knew no bounds as the empire grew and grew. The head office was still based at Birmingham but the main impetus was at Oakamoor.

The growth in demand outstripped supply in Widnes, Oakamoor and even the latest factory at Sutton in Lancashire. The decision to purchase a Greenfield site at Froghall was made in 1890 and the plant was in operation by 1891. At their peak Bolton's had five production sites, Broad Street in Birmingham, Oakamoor, Froghall, Widnes and Sutton.

Alfred died in 1901 and was replaced by his sons, Charles, Thomas, Frances and a son-in-law, Peter Bearblock. The four did not have the best of luck. The years leading up to the first world war brought severe restrictions. British cable makers were forced out of Europe by the growth of tariff protection and the American market was becoming more competitive.

Around 1882, Alfred had formed an alliance with the Callender Wire Company who agreed to make Bolton's their principle supplier. In 1902 Thomas Callender was invited to join the board of Thomas Bolton, and shortly afterwards the firm was reorganised and became a limited company.

Callenders were, first and foremost, salesmen. This fitted in very well with the technical ability of Bolton's, but they soon became the dominant partner. In the 1950s, the copper works of Thomas Bolton and Sons at Froghall was the most important centre in the UK for the manufacture of copper wire and alloys, and perhaps the problems awaiting them could not have been foreseen, but a loss of work from British Railways, a decision by the Post Office to change from overhead wires to underground cables, and the merging of Callenders with British Insulated Cable to form BICC all hit Bolton's. Wire drawing went to the BICC plants at Prescot and Erith, leaving Bolton's with no option but to reduce capacity at Froghall.

BICC was now able to make Bolton's a wholly owned subsidiary. With Oakamoor gone and the buildings facing demolition, the Froghall works concentrated on its copper alloys. When BICC eventually sold their interest in the works in the 1980s there were still 800 people working there, but the next few years saw a continuous process of reduction and what remains now is a minute fraction of the original business. Indeed most of the large Froghall site now looks set for housing.

THE VILLAGE

As the brass and copper industry expanded so did the Oakamoor works of Thomas Patten, even more so after the arrival of Alfred Bolton. The 'waste-land' of Oakamoor began to have its own community as employees of the Caldon Canal Company and the Churnet Valley Railway joined the employees of the Brass and Copper Works in putting down roots.

The 17th century farmhouses no longer seemed remote as workers cottages were built in the bottom of the valley and directors and managers houses were built in selected spots overlooking the village. Public houses, schools, church and chapels, shops and trades of all description followed.

The church was built by Trubshaws of Great Haywood, and completed

The Lodge, owned by Bolton's, and the home of the Bearblocks until the early 1950s when it was demolished.

in 1832. It was consecrated as a Chapel of Ease by the Bishop of Coventry and Lichfield on August 18th. Thomas Patten and family contributed towards the costs with a donation of £100 plus the land and the stone for the church. The Patten family also provided the organ and the bell.

The assistant Curate, John Cotterill noted the lack of a village school. Lord Shrewsbury had built a school-room a short distance away from the village but the curriculum was based on Catholicism. It was deemed by Cotterill and the Rector of Cheadle, the Rev. Delabere Pritchet, that a protestant school was an urgent requirement. Pritchet, by linking together the need for both a church and a school was able to obtain funds from the National Society. Conveniently, the land on which the church was to be built follows a steep incline and by using this to advantage, a school-room was built beneath the first floor of the church. Oakamoor had a church school in every sense of the word.

The architect, J.P. Pritchet, of York was a nephew of the Rector of Cheadle. In the upper Church he included the unusual feature of a three light, straight headed perpendicular window. The east window is of four lights under a four-centred arch. The Tower, to the west, follows the traditional style of church architecture. Fittingly, a memorial inside the church is inscribed to John Horatio Cotterill, the assistant Curate from Cheadle.

In 1864, Oakamoor was granted its own Ecclesiastical Parish and the Chapel of Ease became an independent village church. But the Church of Holy Trinity was not alone in administering the gospel. Primitive Methodism spread from the bleak outcrops of Mow Cop to the Staffordshire Moorlands. Camp meetings became a regular feature during the early 1800s and Ramshor Common (Ramshorn) was a popular venue, close to the villages of the Churnet Valley. Many of the local dissenters would have walked to Ramshor to hear the great William Clowes preach there in 1810. Inspired by the growing following, the Ramshorn Circuit was opened in 1812.

It was common for local dissenters to allow their houses to be used as a meeting place for the new religion. Such houses had to be registered under the appropriate Act of Parliament and several houses in and around Oakamoor did so. The Old Furnace farmhouse was used for meetings in 1830 and in 1838 Richard Wilson opened his house in The Square for use as a meeting house for the Primitive Methodists. Wilson appears to have been a man of great courage and stood by his convictions. Two local ladies of distinction were particularly vociferous against him and the persecution made Wilson's life a misery.

Eventually, rather than give up his faith, Richard moved away to Holywell in North Wales. Holywell's gain was Oakamoor's loss for Wilson was a highly skilled man and a key worker in the art of wire drawing. When Bolton's took over the Oakamoor works it was evident that certain skills were in short supply and Alfred Bolton was a man sympathetic to the Methodist cause. He lost no time in asking Richard Wilson to return and resume his duties in the employ of Thomas Bolton and Son.

Camp meetings were still being held at Jimmy's Yard near the centre of the village and the need for a permanent home was pressing. Oakamoor went from one extreme to the other - in the space of a few years three chapels were built, the Ebenezer Methodist Chapel in 1859, the Wesleyan Chapel on Carr Bank in 1860 and a large room behind the present Admiral Jervis provided by Alfred himself. He appointed a Chaplain in 1868, the Rev. John Mills, followed in 1872 by the Rev.

On Sunday next,
JULY 8, 1888,

A

CAMP MEETING
WILL BE HELD

NEAR THE WESLEYAN CHAPEL,

HARPER'S GATE,
COMMENCING AT
HALF-PAST TWO AND HALF-PAST SIX,
TO BE CONDUCTED BY

Mr. Thomas Geary,
JOYFUL NEWS EVANGELIST;
ADDRESSES MAY BE EXPECTED BY

Messrs. J. MORTON, REDFERN, VIGRASS, HEATH, and others.

The Friends will procession through the village at half-past Five to the place of meeting.

Camp meetings were commonplace in the Moorlands through the 19th century.

Charles Denman, whose fiancé was given the position of governess to the Bolton children at Moorcourt at a salary of £120 per annum.

Charles Denman and his wife became an integral part of the Oakamoor scene and eagerly embraced Alfred's idea of a new 'Mills Chapel' in 1876. By 1878, the chapel was built and in regular use by the workforce. When Alfred died in 1901 it was renamed the Memorial Free Church. The Rev. Charles Denman dedicated his life to the Church and to the people of Oakamoor. He died in 1920 at the age of 73, having served the village for 46 years.

The Church of Holy Trinity continued in its dual role of school and church until 1856 when a second National School was built a few yards away from the church tower. This was knocked down in 1944, but had long been replaced by the Mills School, previously known as the Silk Mills School.

The population of Oakamoor grew rapidly with the copper works. With it approaching seven hundred, the new National School was soon bursting at the seams. Alfred Bolton, in 1871, opened the Mills School in an unused factory building in Mill Street. For years the school was used by factory employees and even embraced silk workers from Broster's silk mill in Leek who travelled to

A camp meeting at Oakamoor.

Oakamoor by train along the Churnet Valley line. The National School was forced into closure through lack of local authority support in 1876, but in 1883, the vicar, Rev. William Cass Greene, attempted to reopen it and started a bitter dispute that lasted for several months. He blamed the closure on Alfred Bolton.

Alfred's school had a formal, authorised structure of education, based on the Quaker system. He appointed a qualified teacher and in 1870 a Miss Graham is recorded as Head of the Silk Mill School. He had started the school in Mill Street with the intention of providing a basic education, but it was far from ideal, so he now had a new Mills School built on the site of Walter Tipper's house that stood close to the Wesleyan chapel on Carr Bank.

Like many of our village schools successive generations passed through its portals. The same will happen to the Valley School, where the children of Oakamoor are now taught, hopefully with less political turmoil and interference than in those early years but, with the same degree of affection and success.

DIMMINGSDALE
You leave the parish of Oakamoor at the point where the Old Furnace Cottages stand on the edge of Dimmingsdale. It is from here that John Higgins takes his guests on their introductory ramble along the ancient pathways that follow Silver Stream towards the Churnet at Lords Bridge, past the Round House in the field to your left, past the fish ponds constructed for the Earl of Shrewsbury and over the stream to join Earls Drive.

This broad track was once used by travellers heading toward Alton Abbey and the occasional mile-post built into the wall testifies to its regular use. Ancient woodlands, now preserved by the Forestry Commission, are home to beech, oak and birch. The birds and animals that frequent these woods and the nearby Hawksmoor Nature Reserve add to the attractions of Dimmingsdale.

Farther on, the drive reaches the mill pond and the stone house that was once the smelting mill. Part of the mill mechanism was incorporated into the internal walls of the house when it was converted to a residential property. The mill pond still serves a useful purpose thanks to Joseph Bamford who purchased it for the JCB Anglers' Club.

This is the half way point of a splendid walk and here, appropriately, the Ramblers Retreat provides a full range of refreshments. How the Ramblers Retreat came to be there is another story of hard work and enterprise. The unusual building was one of two gate-houses that controlled the access into the private woodlands used by the Earl of Shrewsbury, hence the name Earls Drive. A similar gate-house, known as Pink Lodge, stands sentinel over another driveway, opposite to the Earls home, Alton Towers. With the demise of the Earls of Shrewsbury at Alton, the estate became neglected. Dimmingsdale became seriously overgrown and was only saved when the estate was put up for sale and sold off in lots. The valley is now managed by the Forestry Commission and controlled clearance and tree replacement maintain the environment we take so much for granted.

The access road between Alton and Oakamoor that passes Lords Bridge and the Ramblers Retreat has long been known as Red Road. The reason for the name is lost in time although the red rocks and iron stone that are exposed by erosion may be the obvious reason. The road was upgraded during the second world war when Italian prisoners of war were commandeered to turn the former greenway into a permanent highway. Dimmingsdale could hardly be called a prison, though!

The gate-house lodges, attributed to Pugin and built around 1810, were also in danger of decay. Both remained empty for several years and even in later years were only occupied occasionally. However, commonsense prevailed and the buildings were sold for residential use. Pink Lodge is now a popular bed and breakfast outlet catering for visitors to the Alton Towers. Nearby stands the 'Chained Oak' tree that has long been the stuff of legends and witchcraft.

The gate-house close to Red Road was occupied until the 1960s. It then stood vacant for more than a decade, until once again it was in danger of serious decay. Enter Gary and Margaret Keeling. The Keelings were attracted to Dimmingsdale and thought of the gate-house more as a home in a beautiful part

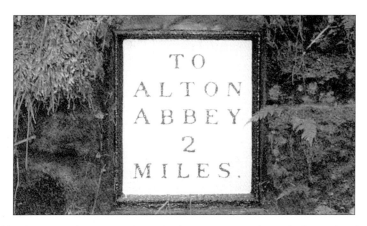

of Staffordshire. They purchased the property in 1978 and after much renovation and restoration, moved in in 1980. Isolated it may have been but the Keelings were not short of company. The area was frequented by workers from the Forestry Commission, conservation groups and ramblers.

It was the ramblers who gave Gary and Margaret the idea and courage to provide teas and light snacks in the living room of their 'new' home. From those humble beginnings in 1981 the Ramblers Retreat was formed. It was a perfect spot for a café and the business went from strength to strength. A car park was provided and toilet facilities were installed. The gardens were extended and over a period of more than twenty years the Ramblers Retreat has become a local institution. It is more than a café these days. The Keelings work seven days a week, providing a comprehensive menu and proving, once again, the old adage 'the harder you work, the luckier you get'.

As unofficial spokesman for Dimmingsdale, Gary is often asked about the nearby smelting mill and the answer takes us again into the history of the Churnet Valley. The Dimmingsdale Smelting Mill was built in 1741, probably for George Talbot, Earl of Shrewsbury. Talbot is recorded as leasing the smelting mill in that year to Thomas Gilbert junior, Anthony Hill and Edward Hill of Shropshire for a period of 99 years. The rent of one shilling per annum seems generous. Gilbert senior was also involved with the mill and left one 24th part of the smelting mill to his son John. The original mill was enlarged and the date inscribed as 1789 ISES above the doorway of the new section.

The mill was primarily involved with the smelting and refining of lead ore that was mined at the lead and copper mine at Ribden, on the outskirts of the Farley parish. The mill was valued at £504 and consisted of the smelting area, the hearth, the refinery, two cottages, a smith's shop and a barn plus the pool and nine acres of land.

The sub-letting continued, with the Gilberts dividing their share between the Duke of Devonshire and four members of the Bill family. The Bills came from Farley and they and the Duke had a vested interest in the lead mines in the Staffordshire Moorlands and the mine at Ecton. A further share was owned by Edward Coyney of Alton.

The lead smelting had a relatively short life and the extension of 1789 must have been more for the grinding of corn than lead smelting. The last reference to lead has to be prior to 1786, as in that year the mill is referred to as the corn mill, formerly a smelting mill, on Alton Common.

In 1841, James Edwards is recorded as a miller living at the smelting mill. In 1851 and 1861, Samuel Coxon is recorded as a miller and farmer. Corn milling thrived for a lot longer than the lead smelting but the families lived in the cottages for many years after both trades had ceased to function. The last occupants had finally moved out by the mid 20th century and in the 1960s the defunct mill was purchased by Joseph Bamford. The mill pond was retained for the benefit of the JCB Angling Club and the mill buildings were sold in the 1980s for conversion into a private property.

FROM INDUSTRY BACK TO NATURE

The smoke and grime that hung over Oakamoor and Froghall, and the hustle and bustle that accompanied the noise of the drop hammers at Consall Forge, affected the immediate surroundings. More widespread was the pollution of local waterways, awash with the dyes and effluent from Leek and Cheddleton.

For centuries there was a strange combination of picturesque scenery and industry, and industry held the whip hand although nature never admitted defeat. But within a century of the departure of the iron and limestone industry, the scars left by a thousand years of man's endeavours have been much disguised by nature. Woodland has reclaimed the hillsides, and birds, animals, flora and fungi are back in force. And these days of course we take a more enlightened view and strive to protect our surroundings.

High above the Churnet, one of its main tributaries, the Coombes Brook, flows through a wooded valley. In 1962, the RSPB purchased 112 hectares of woodland, pasture and hay meadow here to provide a sanctuary for wildlife. The 2005 assessment produced an impressive list of species, including 129 birds, 29 mammals, 1,100 beetles, 1,400 flies, 509 butterflies and moths, 376 plants and 197 fungi. And no, I do not know how they count them all.

The shaded habitat serves to keep the swift flowing brook chilly, even in the height of summer. Not that it deters local children from sampling its delights as they brave the pools that form in the lower reaches. In the bottom of the valley, where the road passes between Basford and Moss Lee, en route to Ipstones, flocks of pewits gather to nest in the marshy grounds that are now covered by man-made fish ponds. Higher up the valley, between Ferney Hill and Apesford, a curlew was more difficult to find, but find it we did, just as we found the sparrowhawk, the jackdaw, the dipper and the kingfisher.

The road between Basford Green and Apesford brings you to the unobtrusive entrance of the RSPB reserve. Nature trails and ancient footpaths meander through woodlands and meadows. Much of the woodland is relatively modern and replaced the indiscriminate tree felling of the early 20th century but, here and there, clumps of oak and other deciduous trees remind you of how the woods of England used to be. Nesting boxes encourage tits, redstarts and pied flycatchers, and in the hedgerows wild flowers and insects proliferate. The meadows are managed to protect butterflies, fungi and wild orchids, and all just far enough away from the main roads to retain its tranquillity.

Like the Coombes Valley Reserve, Consall Nature Park is a low key place. No fanfares announced its formation and signs to it are few. Even so, it attracts many visitors, for its popularity is its accessibility and its proximity to Consall Forge, the canal and the Black Lion public house. The park itself contains attractive walks of various degrees of difficulty. Visitors should be aware that it is a nature park and that wildlife comes first. Dogs must be kept on their leads and children need to be supervised outside of the picnic area. Large ponds attract dragonflies, hoverflies, newts and fish. Grass snakes and adders usually confine themselves to the woodland or the undergrowth but occasionally, in a quiet spot, you may spot them basking in the sun. For the bird lover, the RSPB has a designated walk at Consall. Simply collect a map at the nature park.

From the car park the track takes you to Consall Forge, the Churnet and the canal. The canal towpath, except in wet weather, offers ideal walks. Go left towards Cheddleton, with a stop at the Boat Inn, just a few miles away, or right towards Froghall, passing the old forge buildings on the way. With a bit of luck, you might even see the steam trains that frequent the Valley.

Froghall also has its own special place in the hearts of local people. Sit on the grass outside the tiny shop by the canal wharf, or walk a couple of hundred yards to the new station built in traditional North Staffordshire Railway architectural style.

There is also a National Trust Reserve at Hawksmoor Wood, between Froghall and Oakamoor. As you walk through the wood, it thins out a little before joining the beautiful Dimmingsdale valley and here nature shares its delights with all and sundry. The area compares favourably with anywhere you could care to mention in the Land, despite its popularity.

COTTON COLLEGE

The beautifully positioned Cotton Hall was the home of the Gilbert family from the 17th century, the agents for the Earls of Shrewsbury. In the 1840s, when the family succession failed, the Talbots, Earls of Shrewsbury, acquired it. It was leased for a short time to Richard Badnall, silk dyer, of Leek. Then in 1846 it was offered to Fathers Faber and Newman, prominent in the catholic circle that took in the Earl of Shrewsbury and Pugin. Pugin designed St. Wilfrid's church, which was built in the grounds of Cotton Hall by 1847.

In 1873 the Sedgeley Park School (founded 1763) moved to Cotton Hall and was renamed St Wilfrid's College, Cotton. The teaching staff were predominantly Catholic priests and much of the ancillary care was in the hands of nuns. By the early 1900s it was known simply as Cotton College and remained as such, and an important small boys boarding school and seminary, until the 1980s, outpunching its weight in sport, the arts and academically.

Although boys came from all over the world it always integrated well with the local community and many local boys went to Cotton, often at concessionary rates. Oakamoor and Cotton villages were enlivened with the return of the boys each term arriving at Oakamoor station, to climb the beautiful wooded walk to the College through Star Wood. The College stood in splendid wooded grounds overlooking the brook and Cotton Dell.

By the early 1980s the College, with around 180 boys, was struggling in a modern accountancy-led world. Gone were the nuns and there were fewer clergy and more lay staff at all levels. It was still an oasis of old world courtesy and endeavour for the boys, at least 50% of whom were foreign nationals, South American, Nigerian, Spanish, French and many more. But times were changing and in the early 1980s the Diocese of Birmingham, who ran the College, recalled most of the remaining priests including Father Austin, the headmaster, and the first lay headmaster arrived.

A frantic period of modernisation, with girl boarders admitted for the first time and a new headmaster's house, could not prevent the inevitable and the College closed in 1987. Anyone who had the privilege to meet Fathers Pargeter and Piercy, Terry Owen or Bridie Sharkey, the matron, in those last few years had a glimpse of extraordinary and completely unselfish service.

The College was now on the open market and was bought by a property syndicate with grand ideas of hotels and health clubs. It remained empty and unguarded for years and was rifled of much of its internal fittings by common antique thiefs. There has been talk of the Beckhams and other celebrities buying this neglected jewel over the years but now in 2005 it is in the hands of the Amos property group who are at least guarding what remains of its treasures.

Cotton College in the 1930s. St Wilfrid's church is far right. The original Cotton Hall is to the left of it with the tower entrance prominent. Further buildings were added in the 1960s and 1980s.

Chapter Eight
Farley

BUNBURY HILL

Even the presence of Alton Towers Theme Park fails to detract from the rural charm of Farley. Despite the weekend traffic and the noise from the Park, the village remains an oasis of calm, a hamlet of stone cottages and fine houses that overlook the meadows above the Churnet Valley. Ironically Farley was at the heart of developments for thousands of years and it is only recently that it has become a backwater. Opinion is divided over the development of the theme park. Those living in the immediate vicinity abhor the noise and the traffic that makes their lives a misery. Others see it as a source of employment and trade.

Stone-age man was probably here. No remains have been found in Farley but evidence abounds around the Peak District and along Farley's northern borders. Stone-age man frequented the caves at Cauldon Lowe and artefacts have been found at Waterhouses. Burial grounds are common in the parish in the form of barrows and tumuli. Around 4000 to 5000 years ago, New Stone-age man left flint arrow heads and polished stone axes which have been unearthed near to Farley.

Five barrows at Three Lows were opened by Thomas Bateman between 1845 and 1850 and a number of human skeletons were found, along with burnt human bones, bone pins, antlers, a barbed arrow head, a flint knife, cinerary urns, flint implements and part of a bronze bracelet.

So abundant is the evidence of Stone-age man around Farley that it could well have had a settled community before the establishment of an Iron-age fort. It was certainly a settlement by the time the Iron-age arrived around 2500 years ago. The Iron-age fort referred to as Bunbury Hill is now almost obliterated by the woodlands planted by the Earl of Shrewsbury. In its day it was a magnificent edifice with defensive earthworks that dominated the Churnet Valley and guarded the eastern extremes of the Staffordshire Moorlands.

Excavations at the hill fort suggest that the site was also used during the bronze age. Once again the conclusion is that Farley was a well populated working village several thousand years ago.

The Romans, on their arrival at Rocester, would have found the hill fort at Bunbury Hill a formidable obstacle to overcome, before they could settle into their military station on the confluence of the Churnet and Dove. They would

A depiction of one of Thomas Bateman's famous barrow diggings in the area.

ARCH OF STALACTITES, CAULDON LOW CAVE.
(Waterhouses Station, North Stafford Railway.)

The caves at Cauldon Lowe were quite a tourist attraction at one time but disappeared
somewhere after the 1930s under the quarrying activity.

have encountered an organised community. Francis Redfern, the Uttoxeter historian, noted *'when Alton Towers was constructed, large quantities of charcoal were noticed below the rampart of the iron-age hill fort'*. This gave rise to speculation regarding the smelting of iron or copper. Redfern may have stumbled across the same charcoal that was later to lead Ms J. Mountain (Keele) to a different conclusion. Her archaeological survey in the 1960s suggested that large amounts of undergrowth and timber were cleared from the original site, and burned, prior to the building of the fort.

Perhaps greater emphasis should be placed on the discoveries around Ribden and Blazing Star, the barrows at Ribden Low, the polished flint axe found at Ribden Moat and the perforated stone axe-hammer found at Ribden Farm. The Romans used lead and Ribden and Ecton are obvious contenders for this and the artefacts found in the various mines and in the remains of ancient industrial sites lead to the conclusion that the copper and iron ore in the Churnet Valley was as precious to our Iron age ancestors as it was to the Saxons, Normans, and the entrepreneurs of the Industrial Revolution.

Farley, no doubt, suffered the same fate as the rest of the country when the Romans arrived. With the Bunbury hill fort subdued, Rocester became the dominant player. Local villages transferred their allegiance and traded with the Romans. The Anglo-Saxons, the Danes and the Normans all passed this way but Alton, its neighbour, slowly became the dominant partner. Although separate villages on either side of the Churnet, they appear to many now as one. The Earls of Shrewsbury did not help. They held title to lands on both sides of the river and had no hesitation in building their grand house and gardens on the site of the hill fort on Bunbury Hill in the village of Farley. Calling it Alton Abbey, and later, Alton Towers, only served to confuse outsiders. With both parishes being under the control of the Shrewsburys and the inhabitants often being employed by them, the two villages settled into an amicable alliance.

Alton is recorded in the Domesday Book as belonging to Iuunar *'with land for two ploughs. It is waste'*. Farley is recorded as belonging to Alward *'with land for one or two ploughs. It is waste'*. 'Waste' to William but nevertheless of value to the people of Farley, for the mines at Ribden and the forge at Blazing Star both fell within the demesne land passed on to the Norman overlords.

THE BILLS
The names of the individuals that fill the void between 1086 and the 15th century are not apparent but the occupant of Farley Hall immediately prior to 1607 is known. Robert Shenton of Farley was the principle landowner. His daughter Elizabeth married Richard Bill of Norbury in 1607. Upon Robert's

death the estate passed to Elizabeth and thence to Richard Bill and the Bills remained at Farley Hall for 350 years.

As would be expected, they left their mark on Farley and their memorial plaques grace the church in Alton. One records the service to his country of Lieutenant Robert Bill who died in Gibraltar in 1780 aged 28 years defending the fortress against the Spanish. There is a plaque to Robert Bill who died in 1751 aged 67, and his wife Lydia. Lydia was the daughter of Robert Hurst of Cheadle Grange (probably the partner of Thomas Patten who started the Cheadle Brass Works in 1734. Hurst died in 1769 aged 75).

The last member of the family to bear the name Bill was Major Charles Fitzherbert Bill MP. He served in the Boer War and the 1914-18 War, and died at Farley in 1955. The name Fitzherbert harks back to the family connections with Norbury.

Hugo Bill who died in the 1914-18 war had a daughter, Pamela, who married Christopher Cliff. The Cliffs left Farley Hall in 1957. The Hall and the estate was purchased by the Bamfords and is currently a home of Sir Anthony and Lady Bamford. The style and architecture of the Hall and the stone cottages owe much to the influence of the Bill family, whilst their current pristine condition are a reflection of the Bamfords' maintenance of their estates.

The Bills were generous benefactors to the people of Farley. Perhaps their most welcome act was the installation of a water supply. The Romans may well have had running water, aqueducts and baths but Britain long relied upon the village pump or the local stream. One such stream or spring supplied the Holly Tree Well for generations as the Farley village water supply. The spring on Beelow Hill produced water of exceptional quality and had never been known to run dry. To Charles Bill the answer was obvious. By arranging for the ground to be excavated down to the underground source, and by channelling that source and other outlets into a reservoir, he was able to accumulate a head of 9,000 gallons of water. From the reservoir the water was gravity fed into every house in the village. It was a remarkable achievement that changed the lifestyle of every parishioner. To say they were pleased is an understatement:

TO CHARLES BILL. ESQ.
BY THE TENANTS OF FARLEY

Keenly sensible of the many blessings which we, as your Tenants, have heretofore enjoyed, none have laid us under greater obligation than the water supply, which, at so great expense and with such disinterestedness, you have this day provided for the village of Farley, whereby are brought to our every home the material comforts of civilisation, and the essentials of health and cleanliness.

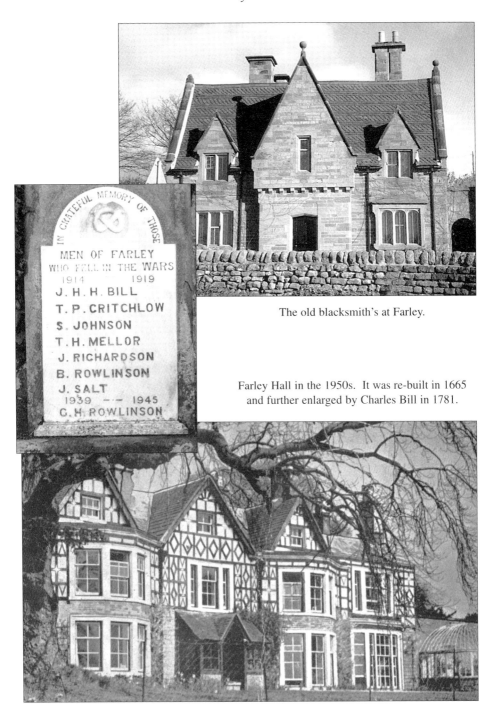

The old blacksmith's at Farley.

Farley Hall in the 1950s. It was re-built in 1665 and further enlarged by Charles Bill in 1781.

We accept this highly useful gift, as an additional proof of your deep concern for our welfare, and for which we hereby desire to record our heart felt gratitude, as also our earnest prayer, that the Divine Providence which has filled your heart with such noble and generous feelings, may long spare you in your career of beneficence and goodwill.

Signed by the parishioners November 21st, 1868

WILLIAM SMITH   RICHARD JACKSON   HENRY WILSON   MARGARET SALT
DAVID FINNEY   MOSES BEARDMORE   DANIEL MELLOR   JAMES GRUNDY
WILLIAM WOOLEY   ELIZTH CHARLESWORTH

The population of the village is small when compared with the parish boundaries. White's directories of 1834 and 1851 give a population of 472 including staff employed at Alton Towers, the Alton Wire Mill, outlying farms and mines plus some who lived and worked in Alton. Farley is '*a neat village, 4 miles E. of Cheadle, its two fairs held on 2nd May and 12th October and now obsolete. Farley Hall is the handsome seat of John Bill Esq which occupies a pleasant eminence.*' Also listed is '*a good travellers' inn*', the Shrewsbury Arms Hotel:

R. ORRELL,

Shrewsbury Arms,

FARLEY.

	M		M		M
Ashbourn	10	Lane End	11	Wolsley Bridge	20
Uttoxeter	10	Burslem	17	Buxton	22
Stafford	20	Stone	14	Matlock	22
Hanley	15	Newcastle	17	Bakewell	24½
Leek	12	Trentham	15	Chatsworth	27½
Cheadle	5	Sandon	14	Derby	22

Earl of Shrewsbury	Alton Towers		
John Bill	Farley Hall		
Edward Bates	Gentleman	Limecrofts	
John Brindley		Colour & Paint Mfr.	Alton Mills.
Wm. Brittain		Gamekeeper	Alton Towers.
Thomas Fradsley		Clerk of Workhouse	Alton Towers.
Joseph Hall		Coal Merchant	Oakamoor.
Joseph Holmes		Shopkeeper	Farley.
Rev. John Pike Jones		Vicar	Alton.
Rt. Wagstaffe Killer Esq			Farley.
John Leigh		Lime Burner	Oakamoor.
Samuel Walker		Beer House	Oakamoor.
Robt. Mellor		Gardener	Alton Towers.
Wm. Mountney		Butcher	Farley.
Richd. Orrell		Victualler	Shrewsbury Arms.
Mrs Sophia Paris		Housekeeper	Alton Towers.

Philip Parker	Butler	Alton Towers.
Rev. Daniel Rock	Chaplain	Alton Towers.
Thos. Weston	Victualler	Talbot. Alton.
Hugh William	Coachman	Alton Towers.
Geo. Winter	Organist	Alton Towers.
Daniel Poyser	Agent	Woodhead Colliery.

Farmers: Briddon, Critchley, Elks, Finney, Flint, Goldsworth, Heaton, Mellor, Ratcliffe, Salt, Shemilt and Tomkinson.

The list includes Finney as a farmer and blacksmith. David Finney, who signed the declaration to Charles Bill in 1868, would have been of the same family.

The directory makes no mention of brickmaking in Farley. There was certainly a brickmaking concern and a substantial one at that. The kiln was set up in 1782 by Charles Bill close to Hillcrest Farm on the land now occupied by the Theme Park. The site was in a field referred to as Brick Kiln Field, indicating that it had been used for brick making before then. The first accounts in 1792 show that 18,000 bricks were made. The following year the figure rose to 55,000. In 1796 92,000 bricks are recorded - and the work seems to have been concentrated into the period May to October. The production of bricks demanded high kiln temperatures which may account for the restriction of production to the summer months.

The brick-maker is referred to as Edward Bennet, whose wages included a sum to cover his attendance at excise sittings, repair costs for the kiln, toll payments and coal purchases. The type of bricks included common and coping bricks and long bricks for flues in '*hot wall*'.

The accounts end after 1796 but the site was still being referred to as Brick Kiln Field on the 1833 Enclosure award for Alton.

THE OLD SMITHY

Farley Road at Alton looking up at the 'new' castle. The site of the old Alton Mill is
seen in the foreground, later a petrol station and café.

'Alton Castle'

Chapter Nine
Alton

ALTON CASTLE

The Stone-age connections mentioned in Farley relate equally to Alton. The Iron-age fort on Bunbury Hill dominated an area devoid of today's boundaries. The Churnet was equally important to the occupants on either side of the valley.

The arrival of the Romans, first at Rocester and then at Chesterton, near Newcastle, brought about a degree of stability, initially by force and then by consent. Total subjugation of the areas along the valleys of the Trent and the Churnet took almost thirty years to achieve. The development of Rocester affected the whole area - and Alton was little more than two miles away.

We are already aware of the Romans use of lead and the possibilities of the Ribden lead mine. The Romans would also have needed timber and stone, both of which were readily available in Alton. There was also the need for pottery, metalworking and more essentially food.

The people of Alton traded with the Romans for almost 400 years and it is more than likely that Roman blood runs through the veins of local descendants. Roman coins have been unearthed in Alton. *The Victoria County History* describes the three gold coins found near Alton castle as: Vespian, 70-77AD; Titus, 71-78AD; Domiton, 81-89AD. More recently, a number of bronze coins have been discovered, dated 250-270 AD, and may have been minted locally.

The roads are difficult to define. Weather permitting, the tracks running along the bottom of the valley, whether to Oakamoor, Cheadle and beyond, or to Denstone, Rocester and Uttoxeter, would have been favoured. From the top of the village, Wheel Lane and Saltersford Lane would have been favoured for the mule carriers. In Denstone it will have crossed the Churnet, hence the addition of 'ford'; Salters indicates a track used by the traders who transported salt. And perhaps the present road between Denstone and Alton has been in use for longer than we realise - a more even route, if a little longer than the salt track.

The Saxon influence is difficult to define, but after the Norman invasion in 1066 and the completion of the Domesday Book, the area was referred to as Alverston, denoting its Saxon heritage. Domesday says that it belonged to Iuuner and passed to King William and thence to his follower, Bertram de Verdun.

The Verduns were subservient to the Earl of Chester who was William's most powerful ally. The Earls of Chester were instrumental in the building of

Ruins of Alton Castle.

many monasteries and their attitude may well have influenced other Norman overlords. Anyway when the Verduns arrived in Alton in 1120 the founding of a house of religion was becoming popular.

In the 12th century Alton was now the centre of attention. The castle, a little of which still remains, was probably the work of Norman de Verdun at the height of his power around 1130. The Church of St Peter is thought to be Norman: the foundation charter of Croxden abbey in 1180 states that the monks were given *'the church of Alverton with all its appurtances'*. The plaque inside the church gives Adam as the first incumbent in 1166, so the church owes its existence to Bertram de Verdun II who was born in 1140 and died in 1192.

A castle and a church point to a sizable village. Croxden Abbey was built at the behest of Bertram, during the latter half of the century.

Bertram's great-grandson, John de Verdun, made extensive alterations to Alton church in the 1260s and the church tower was added in the late 13th or early 14th century. The chancel was rebuilt in the early 16th century by John Hopton, the 24th abbot of Croxden who was appointed in 1519.

Despite John de Verdun's and Hopton's efforts, the church was allowed to deteriorate during the centuries that followed. In 1830, the Archdeacon of Stafford authorised a restoration project that resulted in virtually rebuilding the church. It included the raising of the floor and the laying of flagstones. The double-decker canopied pulpit was removed and the pews replaced and rearranged. The medieval oak roof was also removed and replaced with a conventional structure of lead, lath and plaster. The south wall was rebuilt, and the exterior wall of the north aisle. A stone screen, between the nave and the chancel, had three arches, a central arch that opened to a flight of steps leading to the chancel. The building work was carried out by Mr Evans of Ellastone (of George Eliot fame) at a cost of £932-18-10. Pevsner says:

St. Peters church has a Norman north arcade cut into by the 14th century west tower. Six bays, round piers, square abice, round double-chamfered arches. The arcade is ruthlessly renewed, the south arcade looks all early 19th century. The exterior with windows pointed on the north, with Y-tracery on the south, confirms that in fact the building was all but rebuilt in 1830. Chancel and south chapel of 1884-5 by J.R. Naylor. Font Octagonal, Perp,

Pevsner's comment *'ruthlessly renewed'* is surely correct but at the time the restoration and renewal suited the purpose and tastes of the people. The church is primarily a place of worship and not a shrine to architecture. *The History of Farley and Alton* (edited by Robert Speake), whilst endorsing Pevsner's view, gives a more sympathetic appraisal. The Norman arches are still in situ, having escaped the restoration of the 1830s.

Further restoration work in 1860 saw the musicians' gallery at the west of the church dismantled. In 1883 a combined vestry and organ was installed, the chancel was re-roofed, the floor relayed, a new chancel arch installed and the tower *'in a dangerous condition'* repaired (it was 14th century after all). The costs were met by Charles Bill of Farley and Colin Minton-Campbell of Rocester.

The Verduns were important members of the court and all powerful around Alton. They held land in Normandy, Ireland, Buckinghamshire, Warwickshire and Leicestershire. With such wealth came responsibilities. Bertram accompanied Richard I on the third crusade, a risky business. He also accompanied Prince John to Ireland, which must have stretched his diplomatic skills to the limit. He was still serving his King and Country when in 1192 he accompanied Richard to the Holy Land and died fighting in the defeat of the Saracens at the capture of the Jaffa.

The influence of the Verduns continued for over 150 years until the demise of the family through the lack of a male heir. The Verduns got around the problem once in 1231 when Nicholas de Verdun died, leaving his daughter, Rohese as his heir. Rohese married Theobald Butler who took the Verdun name and so retained the Verdun estates through a degree of duplicity.

In 1316 the problem arose again after a later Theobald died at Alton castle leaving three daughters but no sons. The Verdun estates were split three ways. His widow, Elizabeth de Burgh received one third which denied her possession of the estates. The remaining two thirds reverted temporarily to the Crown, pending the coming of age or the marriage of the female heir, Joan. In due course Joan married Thomas de Furnival of Sheffield and Worksop in 1318.

The years between Theobald's death and Joan's marriage saw unprecedented problems at Alton. The King's custodian saw fit to line his own pockets from the Verdun estate. Watchful friends and old neighbours were quick to rally to prevent Roger Dammory from further exploiting the Verdun girls, especially Thomas Barynton of Creighton, near Crakemarsh. Barynton took the castle by force and removed Dammory. It took the intervention of the King and the sheriff of Stafford to bring matters to a solution and Barynton frustrated Dammory long enough until the marriage of Joan.

The Furnivals were not a popular replacement as they concentrated their efforts on their Sheffield and Worksop estates. Upkeep of the castle and estate went into decline and in 1316 the castle was described as ruinous. The castle was rebuilt, probably by the Earls of Shrewsbury, because the castle was intact when it was taken over by the Royalists during the civil war. It eventually fell to Sir John Gell, the Parliamentarian, in 1642. The confrontation left Alton castle a ruin again from which it never recovered.

The old castle ruins drawn in 1731.

THE TALBOTS

With the Furnivals absentee landlords, Alton, by now a borough, was in decline. It only began to recover when the Talbots married into the Furnivals. The Talbots also came over with William the Conqueror. By the 14th century, their influence had spread to many parts of the country, including Shropshire. John

Talbot (1384-1453) became the first Earl of Shrewsbury and over the following two centuries his descendants acquired much land and estates through marriage or purchase including large tracts of Staffordshire and Derbyshire.

The Talbots now married into the dynasty created by Bess of Hardwick, and so inherited even greater wealth. Charles, the 15th Earl, took a particular delight in the countryside around Alton and decided to transform the area north of the Churnet into 600 acres of splendour. In 1814, he moved into Alton Lodge where he lived until his death in 1827.

Charles was succeeded by his nephew, John, who was equally inspired by Alton. He left his home in Heythrop and moved to Alton to continue the transformation. John was an ambitious catholic and, in addition to his interest in the parklands, he set out to encourage his beliefs in the area. John's friendship with Augustus Pugin and Ambrose Phillips, both catholics, is evident in the architectural gems financed by him locally.

Alton Lodge was extended beyond recognition and eventually became known as Alton Towers. But Pugin's influence is seen to its best in the Church of St Giles in Cheadle. John financed the building of St Giles and also the building of St Mary's in Uttoxeter.

Alton Towers, from the Terrace.

John also transformed the castle site on the opposite side of the valley. He, Pugin and Phillips decided to build a hospital for the aged, along with a guild hall and a presbytery, on the rocky castle heights above the Churnet, to bring care and education to the village. John also contributed to education elsewhere in the area but it was in Alton that he really left his mark. The village once again found itself the seat of power. Education was applied, employment was provided and the area flourished.

At this point an expensive court case over the succession took its toll and although the Talbots were still wealthy, the Shrewsbury dynasty was never the same again. A great sale resulted in the loss of fine paintings and valuable heirlooms and the internal splendour of Alton Towers was lost.

Charles John, the 19th Earl, married Theresa Cockerell in 1855, and was a popular

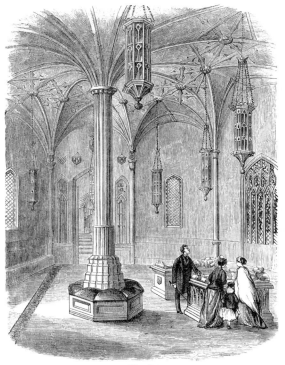

The Octagon.

figure in Alton and Staffordshire. It was he who first opened the gardens at Alton Towers to the general-public. By working in conjunction with the North Staffordshire Railway Company, the Earl not only attracted visitors to the gardens, but also received a payment from the railway company in return for the number of extra passengers.

The gardens remained open until about 1900 when the North Staffordshire Railway Company stopped the fares concession. It was reopened after the First World War by Charles Henry, the 20th Earl. When he died in 1921, he was succeeded by his grandson John, who was only seven at the time and the estate was put up for sale. The house and gardens were purchased by a company who turned them into a tourist attraction, although more for the splendid gardens and the Pugin inspired house than the excitement of today's theme park.

The estate on the other side of the valley, the convent, the school, the priest's house, the hospital and the Catholic church, were purchased for the parish and the Roman Catholic Church. Remarkably, the majority of the money came from the generosity of one man, W.D. Turnbull.

So ended the day to day involvement of the Earls of Shrewsbury with the

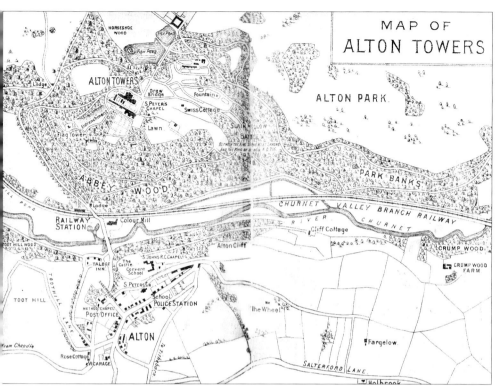

A plan of Alton Towers and Alton produced for Heywood's tourist booklet about 1890.

village of Alton. The ownership of Alton Towers now passed through several hands, including the government, who took over the estate on behalf of the War Office from 1939-1945. The army moved in and erected a camp of wooden huts in the walled garden to the south of the hall. After the army left in the 1950s the estate was taken over by a leisure group and has slowly developed into the present day Alton Towers Theme Park.

THE MILLS

As the village developed under the care of the Verduns, Furnivals and Talbots, the industrial part of the village also developed. The everyday trades of carpenter, wheelwright, blacksmith, mason and builder, the shopkeeper, the cobbler and the innkeeper, all employed people in the village.

The castle and the church sat high above the valley, aloof to the day to day affairs of the population in the valley below. The Churnet, where the corn mill was driven by the water wheels, was the source of power for centuries. The mill was used for numerous other trades and was still in use in the early days of the

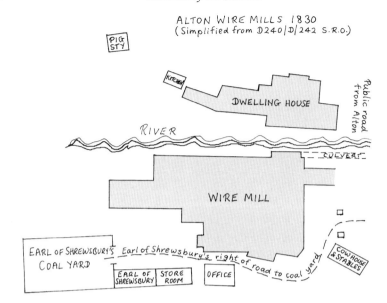

ALTON WIRE MILLS 1830
(Simplified from D240/D/242 S.R.O.)

PIG STY

KITCHEN

DWELLING HOUSE

Public road from Alton

RIVER

CULVERT

WIRE MILL

EARL OF SHREWSBURY'S COAL YARD

Earl of Shrewsbury's right of road to coal yard

EARL OF SHREWSBURY

STORE ROOM

OFFICE

COW HOUSE & STABLES

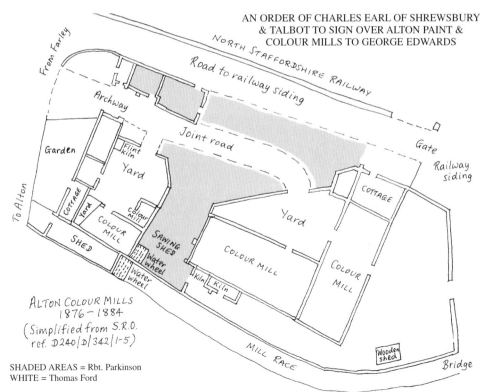

AN ORDER OF CHARLES EARL OF SHREWSBURY
& TALBOT TO SIGN OVER ALTON PAINT &
COLOUR MILLS TO GEORGE EDWARDS

From Farley

NORTH STAFFORDSHIRE RAILWAY

Road to railway siding

Archway

Joint road

Garden

Flint kiln

Yard

Gate

Railway siding

To Alton

COTTAGE

Yard

COLOUR MILL

Colour Mill

SHED

SAWING SHED

Water wheel

Water wheel

Yard

COTTAGE

COLOUR MILL

Kiln Kiln

COLOUR MILL

ALTON COLOUR MILLS
1876 – 1884
(Simplified from S.R.O.
ref. D240/D/342/1-5)

MILL RACE

Wooden shed

Bridge

SHADED AREAS = Rbt. Parkinson
WHITE = Thomas Ford

20th century. Three mills, all water driven, occupied the skills of local men. One, at Dimmingsdale, has already been covered in an earlier chapter. The other two were in the village itself. The Cotton Mill, situated a few hundred yards down stream from the Alton to Farley road, had a limited life and little remains of its existence except for a few of the stones that formed the weir.

By far the most successful was the mill situated next to the Farley road by the stone bridge that spans the Churnet. This mill had a long and varied life over a period of over 800 years - and a mill must have been in existence prior to 1181, when it was recorded as belonging to Croxden Abbey. From that time, the mill is referred to frequently, whether by the chroniclers of Croxden Abbey or by various Lords of the Manor or by the mill operator himself. It is also plain that the mill was reasonably substantial and not a single wheel enterprise. A valuation for the Furnivals in 1327 noted *'Two water mills under one covering, for which the Abbot of Croxden gets forty shillings annually'*.

After the dissolution of the monasteries, the mill was leased to Francis Basset and by 1566 it was in the possession of the Earl of Shrewsbury, who leased it for twenty-one years to Henry Whiston and William Woodward.

The mill was used to grind corn and it was referred as such in the sale details of 1647 drawn up for John Talbot, the 10th Earl. The mill was later leased by Charles, Duke of Shrewsbury, to Robert Bill for a period of ninety-nine years and the biggest change in the history of the mill occurred under his tenure. He entered into an agreement with Thomas Patten of Cheadle Brass Co in 1734 and, in doing so, became a partner, along with Robert Hurst, John Watkins and Thomas Barker, in the Alton Wire Mill. Conversion from corn mill to wire mill involved substantial building work.

Thomas Patten used the Alton wire mill from 1734 until 1828 when the business was transferred to Oakamoor. Many references are made to corn grinding at Alton mill, even during the Patten era but it is more than likely that the references are to other mills. Dimmingsdale and Holbrook mill were both capable of grinding corn.

Relations of the famous canal engineer, James

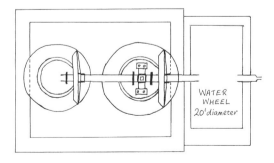

Sketch from S.R.O. Ref. D240/E(A)/2/14A (Simplified)
PLAN OF 2 PANS FOR ALTON FLINT MILL 1829

WATER WHEEL 20'diameter

ESTIMATE FOR ALTON FLINT MILL 1829
Waterwheel 20ft high, 7ft wide 2 pans, 1 12ft diam., 1 11ft diam £620.00

Brindley, lived at Alton and worked as managers of the wire mill. Joseph Brindley worked at the mill up to his death in 1820 and the last member of the Brindley family to work there was John, who was made redundant in 1828, when the lease expired and the business was transferred to Oakamoor. John continued in business at Alton as a colour manufacturer for a few years but was unsuccessful and declared bankrupt in 1834.

Having gone from corn mill to wire mill to colour mill, it now went to paper manufacturing. The first reference appears in the census returns of 1841 when Joseph Smith is noted as *'Paper Manufacturer employing nine papermakers'*. By 1851 the control appears to have passed to James and Sarah Mather, who came from Middleton. The Mathers had six children, two of whom, Robert and John worked for the company. Also included are five other papermakers, an engine man, a paper finisher and nine labourers.

The next census, in 1861, records Martin Rourke as *'Paper Manufacturer with twenty-one employees'*. He took over the papermaking business from the trustee after the death of Mather and continued until papermaking ceased in 1867.

Papermaking was probably the last of the industries to utilize the mill in its entirety. Later records point to a multitude of uses on the same site. The sketches illustrated, outline the mill layout in 1830, just after the departure of Thomas Patten, and the layout in 1876 after the paper mill had closed. The map relates to the Earl of Shrewsbury passing the premises to George Edwards of Stoke-on-Trent. Edwards owned or leased several colour mills in North Staffordshire and was a major supplier to the pottery industry.

The sawing yard appears to be a separate business with its own water wheel. Later, the mill was used by a stone cutting company and the buildings facing the main road between Alton and Farley served their time as a café and a petrol station. Today, the almost derelict site is crying out to be used again.

RELIGION

In the village itself, a bygone age can be found in the form of stone buildings, converted shops and Methodist chapels. The stone jail, in the centre of the village, is hardly indicative of large scale crime, and the chapels are still used. Their quiet and peaceful demeanour does little to remind people of the religious zeal that brought about their existence. The Catholic church owes its existence to the Earls of Shrewsbury who did much for the recovery of Catholicism, and the Anglican church, with its long history, had served the village for many centuries. It was the failings of the Catholic and Anglican Churches that fed the desire for change and the advent of the non-conformist movement. Alton followed the pattern of other villages and towns in embracing the principles of John Wesley. It witnessed the same pressures and indignities to the early non-conformists who opposed the rulings of the established church.

William Walker, who lived at Grove House on Smithy Bank, opened his house to the Primitive Methodists in January 1812. Hugh Bourne was among the petitioners. Grove House served its purpose for fourteen years when the Primitive Chapel on New Road was built, distinguished by its red bricks and dressed stone plinth that supports the tiled roof. A porch was added towards the end of the 19th century using brick produced at John Fielding's brickworks at Battlesteads. It did not stand the test of time and had to be rebuilt in 1933.

The Chapel proved a popular venue with attendances of over one hundred. The house attached to the chapel was used first by the resident minister and later by the caretaker until it was sold in 1988 and converted into a private residence.

Religious issues were never fully resolved. More chapels were built, each with allegiance to its own particular interpretation of the Wesleyan principles. The Providence Chapel held sway for many years before being converted to a private house. The Wesleyan Chapel, situated in the High Street, offered a direct challenge to the village church by standing opposite the gates of St. Peter. It was built in 1856 and closed, in 1959. The Primitive and Wesleyan Methodists were reunited in 1932 but even then, each chapel continued to hold a separate service and it was not until 1959 that the congregations came under one roof, hastened by dry rot in the roof of the Wesleyan chapel.

Alton certainly has had its fair share of spiritual guidance. The Catholic Church was part of the 'castle' complex instigated by the Earl of Shrewsbury and influenced by Pugin and Ambrose Phillips. The hospital was in reality a sanctuary for poor children, who were nursed to good health and then educated in the catholic faith. Acceptance to the hospital school would have been a great privilege during the early years of the 19th century. Today the school forms part of the parish church dedicated to St. John, whilst the education of catholic children takes place in more suitable accommodation. The convent building remains to remind us all of just how great an architect, Pugin was.

The whole area, with its medieval appearance, on a site once occupied by the Lords of the Manor, remains a splendid surprise to the unsuspecting visitor. Walk a few hundred yards along Red Road, by the side of the Churnet, turn around and look up towards the castle. The view is stunning. Quite why the local authority allowed the monstrous brick-built block next to the castle is beyond comprehension.

Denstone village
school

The War Memorial looking
onto Denstone College's
playing fields.

The Tavern at Denstone.

Chapter Ten
Denstone and Quixhill

A FORD ON ANCIENT ROUTES

Denstone did not become a parish until 1861, before which it was linked with Rocester or Alton. The 'new' parish included nearby Quixhill and Prestwood.

The name Denstone, Dens-Ton, suggests its Saxon heritage. Its detailed history is perhaps best left to local historian Tom Goode, whose little book on the village is to be found in the archives section of Uttoxeter library.

Denstone was part of the Saxon kingdom of Mercia in the years before the Norman Conquest and was under the control of Iwar, the Lord of the Manor. It is reasonable to assume that the land was sufficient to provide a living for Iwar and his family. In Domesday, Denstone had 360 acres of ploughland and it may be that Iwar held other lands, for both Quixhill and Prestwood had contentious squabbles over land rights during the years that followed.

After Iwar was dispossessed of his lands by the Normans, the hamlet passed to the King, and then to his trusted followers, the Verduns.

Denstone was being farmed when Richard was fighting the Crusades, by one Geoffrey de Denstone at Manor Farm. Both Croxden Abbey and Rocester Abbey were well established by then and from their records we discover mention of Denstone in 1261: *'The Abbot of Rocester sued Robert de Okeover and Margaret, his wife for entering his wood at Northull (Barrow Hill) and destroying the herbage and pannage'.* We are also told that Walter the Abbot was represented by his canon, Roger de Clifton, and that Robert de Okeover was represented by Everard de Denstone.

The water mills on the Churnet are recorded here. In 1254, Robert de Waterfall claimed possession of a water mill at Denstone, and in 1272, we learn of the death of Geoffrey of Quixhill who was crushed by a stone at the mill. Whether Quixhill and Denstone mill were one and the same is impossible to say but it does seem likely when you consider that Rocester, just a mile down stream also had water mills on the Churnet and the Dove.

It would be easy to think of Denstone as rural backwater but close as it was to Rocester, and also the ancient saltway and the greenway to Ellastone, a considerable amount of traffic would pass through the village. Enough to keep the ale houses busy. Both Romans and packhorses would have forded the Churnet at its shallowest level between Denstone and Quixhill. Quixhill Bridge was not built until the 19th century. The building of this stone bridge would have been quite an event. Most of the stone bridges over the Churnet were built during the 16th and 17th centuries but the ford at Quixhill had coped with local traffic. Quixhill Bridge is a listed building described as *'early 19th century, of stone ashlar construction, three arches with chamfered voussoirs spanning the Churnet. The central arch is large and flanked by shallow buttresses and each stone of the vaults is inscribed with the mason's mark'*.

On the outskirts of Quixhill a couple of period properties are still in use today.   Both are listed buildings and are excellent examples of their kind. Manor Farm is described as follows:

'....dated 1708, but incorporates the remains of an earlier house. Coursed, 1708 squared and dressed large stone blocks with ashlar dressings; clay tile roof with coped verges on shaped kneelers; coursed and squared stone integral end stack, brick stack to N.W corner of main range. Main three bay range of 1708 aligned NW-SE. The house was extended and altered several times during the 19th and early 20th century. The timber-framed walls of 1708 that define the central bay and the timber-framed smoke hood to the NW of the first floor are probably the remnants of the earlier building. Was the earlier building the one occupied by Geoffrey de Denstone at the time of Richard I?'

Manor Farm

Lower House, opposite Manor Farm, is dated 1630:

'Coursed and squared large stone blocks with ashlar dressings; clay tile roof with coped verges; central brick stack. Two room lobby-entry plan. Two

storeys and gable lit attic; two windows; two light flat faced mullioned windows replacing earlier ones; small single light fire window to left of centre with rebated surround and straight hood mould; central gabled porch with moulded coping, and returned hood mould to shallow cambered arch with boarded door, date stone above; moulded eaves cornice. Both gable ends similar fenestration, chamfered mullioned windows in rebated surrounds, all with straight hood moulds, that to attic has three lights, those to ground and first floor have four.'

Lower House

The Earl of Shrewsbury made Quixhill the eastern entrance to his Alton estate and the gates to Quixhill Park still stand although now the access to the JCB Test Centre. The gates were part of a splendid entrance built in the early 19th century, a triumphal arch, gates, railings and two lodges. It is described as *'ashlar built into a chaste neo-classic design ...a central rounded archway with raised keystone, springing from Tuscan pilasters and flanked by flat headed*

The Denstone entrance to the Alton Estate via Quixhill Park, showing one of the lodges.

arches on Tuscan columns ...wrought iron gates completed the main central arch and flanking each side of the triple arch entrance were wrought iron railings, twenty yards in length and bearing fleur-de-lys crested standards. There were two stone lodges linked on either side by the railings'.

CANAL & RAILWAY

The 19th century brought far-reaching changes to Denstone. The Caldon Canal was extended in 1811 from Froghall to Uttoxeter. The canal passed through Denstone, close to Quixhill Park, where it had its own wharf and loading bay. The village pubs did good trade. The Shoulder of Mutton looked after the navvies as did the Tavern and the Royal Oak. The village blacksmith also benefited from the extra work, shoeing the stocky horses that pulled the barges. But the life of the canal was relatively short, closing as it did in 1849.

The Churnet Valley Railway followed the route of the canal extension and replaced it. Denstone had a stationmaster and a compliment of staff, plus a busy goodsyard, and when Denstone College was built, parents and pupils made frequent use of the station and a ride to Alton Towers cost but a few pence.

The factories at Rocester, Oakamoor, Cheddleton and Leek were now an easy journey away and a change of train at Uttoxeter put Derby, Burton and Stafford within reach. The coming of the railway and the growing population led to parish status, a period of great change and great patronage.

The Heywoods arrived in the area in 1839, when they moved to Doveleys and took on the role of Lord of the Manor. They were generous benefactors and took a special interest in the welfare of the village. Through them Denstone received its first water supply to the houses owned by the Heywoods and to a series of roadside taps strategically placed in the village. The change from a village pump, or a well in the garden or field, to a tap that never ran dry was a wonderful event. The people of Denstone contributed generously to the erection of a village cross and drinking fountain, inscribed thus, *'This cross is erected by the parishioners and friends, AD1900 to the glory of God and in memory of Sir Thomas Percival Heywood, baronet and of his work in the parish of Denstone'.*

The Heywoods also supported the school and the church. The incumbency of the church was in their hands. The fine group of buildings that include the church, the school, the coach house, the stables and the churchyard cross are the work of the architect, G.E. Street, whose work was much admired by Heywood. The Church Hall is also attributed to Street and all the buildings relate to what must have been a glorious period in the 1860s. One can only imagine the anticipation felt by the village as the buildings grew day by day before their eyes. The school would have been an up to date and valuable addition to village life.

DENSTONE COLLEGE

Even more significant were the developments in the 1860s that led to the establishment of Denstone College. Nathaniel Woodward established a number of schools based upon a religious foundation and greatly admired by those who wished to encourage a system with a blend of the spiritual and the academic. A group of Midland Anglicans wanted to replicate his principles locally and one, Sir Percival Heywood, contributed a fifty acre site at Denstone for the school.

With the support of Bishop Lonsdale of Lichfield and his successor, Bishop Selwyn, the foundations were laid in 1868. The buildings, designed in the Gothic style by William Slater and R.H. Carpenter, were in the form of an H with the two open quadrangles named Lonsdale and Selwyn. The first section, which included the 'great schoolroom' was opened within the year.

Initially, 47 pupils enrolled at a fee of 34 guineas a year. The school quickly gained popularity under Rev. W.B. Stanford, the first headmaster (1875-78) and his successor, the Rev. D. Edwardes (1878-1903). A library was opened in 1881, a chapel in 1887, a dining room in 1891, laboratories and a gymnasium in 1900 and a sanatorium in 1901. By 1902 there were 303 pupils.

Denstone's first university award was achieved in 1876 and by the 1890s scholarships were won on a regular basis. The curriculum included German, Spanish, Hebrew, chemistry, physics, biology, geology, book-keeping, shorthand and typing. Games flourished. A fives court was opened in 1876, and a bathing pool. Rugby arrived in 1884, and compulsory cricket in 1887.

The Great Schoolroom at Denstone.

Rev. F.A. Hibbert (1905-1919) also achieved great success. In 1913, the laboratories were enlarged and electric lighting installed, and by the end of his tenure the number of pupils was 330. Post-war austerity and the depression hit the College and numbers reduced until, in 1931, T.A. Moxon arrived. By 1936, attendance and academic standards were once again improving and Smallwood Manor, in Hanbury, was leased in 1937 to house the Preparatory School.

The post-war austerity of the 1950s again saw a fall in numbers but once again an inspired headmaster came to the rescue. Under B.M.W. Trapnell (1957-68) a new boarding house was built, land acquired for an extra sports field, new laboratories completed and an indoor swimming pool and athletic track provided. Better teachers were attracted by the provision of school owned houses in the village and a headmaster's house was built in 1964. He raised standards and pupil numbers - and in 1963 abolished fagging.

And still today, Denstone College continues to play a leading role in education as one of the best small public schools.

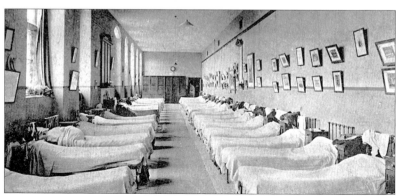

Chapter Eleven
Rocester

A HUB OF ACTIVITY

Nowadays a a very working class looking town set in an area of rural tranquility, Rocester has seen great activity over the past 2000 years. The land bordering the Churnet and the Dove has supported settlements for longer than history records but Rocester as a town arrived with the Romans. When Agricola became governor of Britain in AD 78, he established control by introducing law and order. To control the occasional uprising, he made a network of roads linking strategically placed centres. Between the cities where the Romans settled, forts were built and manned by Roman infantry. Around these forts locals gathered to trade, and many serfs or paid artisans were used by the Roman settlers.

Rocester was situated midway between Little Chester (Derby) and Chesterton (Newcastle-under-Lyme), the site on the confluence of the Churnet and Dove, ideally placed to keep locals in check and to provide a pleasant stopping off point for travellers. Agricola proved to be an excellent governor. Most of his plans were accomplished in the first decade of his governance and it is likely that Rocester would have been established in these earlier years, if only because of the importance of Little Chester and Chesterton. Rocester will be one of a unique few to celebrate its second millennium around 2065.

The Romans left their mark and the site of the fort and its surroundings have been excavated many times, although the unwise siting of the new cemetery curtails future excavations. Even so, enough has been achieved to form an idea about life in Rocester 2000 years ago, much of which is to be found in *A History of Rocester* (2003) and in the *Roman Excavation Project 1986* carried out by Ian Ferris of Birmingham University. A copy of the excavation project's findings is held in the archival section of Uttoxeter library.

Ian Ferris and Malcolm Cooper, with the financial support of Sir Anthony Bamford of JCB, were responsible for the most detailed excavations to date, although as far back as 1792 artefacts were being unearthed. Redfern, in his *History of Uttoxeter* quotes many 'finds' over a period of a 150 years. In the mid-20th century, the boys of Oldfield School dug a number of trenches in the Abbey fields and discovered artefacts. It was perhaps just as well that greater controls were introduced. A professional archaeologist, Dr Graham Webster, carried out a 'dig' in 1961 and to Webster we owe the first genuine description

The Seal of Rocester Abbey

Celtic axe-head
found near
Rocester

Roman coins excavated at Rocester

of the Roman fort. Among the most important of Webster's conclusions are:

1. A late 1st century earthen rampart inside - a series of trenches for the sleeper beams of timber buildings. These were interpreted as part of the Roman fort.

2. Sometime after AD160 a second rampart was built along the line of the original. It was suggested that this might form part of the defences of a civil settlement.

3. Part of the second bank was cut away to allow the insertion of a stone wall, contemporary with which was a quarry pit of AD 280 or later.

4. This pit was overlain by a tilling layer containing 4th century pottery.

5. This, in turn, was overlain by a marked horizon of burning, which yielded a late Saxon strap end, late 9th century, and a number of knife blades.

6. In the medieval period the area was used for dumping stone rubble.

The discovery of the second rampart raises more questions than it answers. It may well be that the fort was not abandoned when the Romans were recalled to their homeland but remained in civil control as a defence of the township during the lawless times that followed.

The excavations in 1985, by Ferris and Cooper and the team from Birmingham University lasted 13 weeks and a 30 x 10 metre area was opened in the new cemetery. Although predominately Roman, a substantial number of later artefacts were discovered, including pottery shards ranging from Roman times through to the 13th century: 111 alloy objects including 31 Roman coins, 1,500 nails and 200 other iron objects, 4,000 shards of pottery of Roman manufacture, 1,000 of medieval date and 2,000 post-medieval. Rocester was a busy commercial town, the most important in the area, easily surpassing Uttoxeter.

The departure of the Romans, after 300 years of steady growth, left many prosperous citizens, between 1000-1200. Perhaps their reliance on the Roman fort and its wealth had generated a false sense of security, for the town entered a steady period of decline. For several centuries the Anglo Saxons dominated, then the Vikings and eventually the Normans. By the Norman conquest, Rocester was a semi-Christian community under the Saxon Earl Alfgar and according to Domesday consisting of: *'1 hide, with all its dependencies. Land for 9 ploughs, in lordship 2. 18 villagers and 10 smallholders with 9 ploughs. A mill at 10s, meadow 20 acres, woodland 1 furlong and as wide. Value before 1066 £4. now £8'.* Uttoxeter was of a similar size and had the same value of £8.

THE ABBEY

Rocester grew little over the next 700 years while Uttoxeter flourished, although the Abbey of St. Mary was founded 1141-46 by Richard Bacon, a nephew of Ranulph, Earl of Chester. Richard appointed Thurston as the first abbot and gave to the abbey, *'the church at Rocester together with the vills of Rocester and East Bridgeford (Notts) and the lands and tenements belonging to them'*. In a second charter we find also *'the chapels of Bradley in the Moors and Waterfall, the vills of Rocester and Combridge and its demesnes, and at Wooton with its appurtenance and liberties in Nothill, Denstone, Quixhill, Roston, Bradley, Waterfall and Calton, plus 8 carucates and 2 bovates of land and the third part of two mills in East Bridgeford'*.

A substantial estate. The Manors of Rocester, Combridge and Quixhill amounted to 26 messuages, 10 cottages, 40 barns, 38 stables, 35 orchards, 400 acres of arable land, 400 acres of meadow, 800 acres of pasture, 20 acres of woodland and 30 acres of furze and heath. Still the abbey pleaded poverty from time to time! Sheep breeding, both for wool and food, was the traditional source of income and with 1,200 acres plus a fulling mill on the Dove and a corn mill on the Churnet, the abbey would have made a handsome living. It appears more a case of mismanagement than misfortune, although the occasional visit of the plague, droughts, floods and famine would mean periods of austerity.

From time to time there were problems with the canons. Indeed, it was not unknown for certain canons to adopt a secular lifestyle if left to their own devices. One, Geoffrey Spagurnel, was despatched to the King's court on business, but was then accused of spending the abbot's money and retaining the documents. Another canon, Richard Foston, was involved in acts of impropriety in the latter part of the 1300s. Foston was a wastrel who roamed the countryside in secular attire, causing mayhem wherever he went. He was arrested for his misdeeds, in 1375, by William de Verney of Denstone, John Basset, Sheriff of Staffordshire, William de Haughton and Thomas de Stafford.

Perhaps this paints an unfair picture of abbey life. There were equally long periods of peace during which the people of Rocester were happy to live side by side with their devout neighbours, and it came as a shock to the village and to the abbey alike when Henry VIII split with the Catholic Church and decided the monasteries were not only allies of Rome, but too rich for their own good.

Local figures loom large in the events of 1538. William Cavendish, who later moved to Doveridge, and Thomas Legh, were the local auditors chosen to assist the receiver for Staffordshire. Cavendish and Legh conducted the surrender of Rocester Abbey and Croxden Abbey and were implicit in the auctions that followed. The Abbot of Rocester, Wylliamum Grafton, signed the deed of surrender on 16th September 1538. The reasonable assumption is that Cavendish and others benefited greatly in the properties they acquired.

Although the abbey had its own church, the village church continued its traditional role, sometimes with the support of the abbot, sometimes not. This led to confrontation on at least one occasion, when the Bishop was called upon to resolve matters. It seems the canons were insisting that the villagers should attend the monastery service. The Bishop ruled in favour of the village.

The church of St Michael survived the events of 1538. The first new incumbent was Thomas Mecocke in 1533 - who was to succeed William Grafton as abbot. The fabric of the church was already over 500 years old then and beginning to show signs of wear. Nowadays the only remaining evidence of the old church is the 12th century cross that stands in the churchyard and the silver gilt cup that is still in use today. The church was rebuilt, almost entirely, in 1871, the main benefactors Mr C.M. Campbell, Sir Percival Heywood, the Houldsworth family, Mrs Dawson and Mrs Webb of Clowneholme.

St Michael's church.

William Trentham purchased the manor of Rocester after the dissolution. The man in the street at the time was somewhat less fortunate and Rocester had its fair share of poverty and deprivation. The Parish Registers show:

1598   A poor woman was buried whose name we know not.
1612   Roger, a beggars son, baptised.
1714   A poor child died in Towne street.

Rocester despatched its paupers to the workhouses in Ipstones and Caverswall and contributed 2s-6d per person for the privilege.

Education in the middle ages was the domain of the privileged. The masses, unable to read and write, relied upon the wisdom of their elders. Some learnt at the hands of the Quakers or the local sage, and the terms 'hedge school' and 'dame school' refer to individuals who taught the fundamentals in the open air or in their own homes. Methodist Sunday schools became important from the late 18th century but it was not until the late 19th century that Britain could claim a system of compulsory education for everyone - a little over 100 years ago.

Rocester, like many other villages, had a church school. Prior to the introduction of secondary education, the children remained at the village school until the age of thirteen, later fourteen years. Rocester again benefited from the largesse of benefactors - Henry Houldsworth is credited with the building of the first proper village school on Ashbourne Road in 1852.

THE MILLS

The industrial revolution, initially harnessing the power of local rivers and later the steam engine, made Britain the most powerful nation on earth. In Rocester, the corn mill that stood close to the Churnet was in regular use until the 19th century, and on the Dove, the water wheels turned the mechanism of the wash pans used by the canons of St. Mary's to improve the sheep wool by the fulling process. But it was the Dove rather than the Churnet that brought mass employment to Rocester. Cotton spinning came to Rocester when Richard Arkwright expanded his empire from Cromford, near Matlock. Arkwright chose the site of an existing mill situated by the Dove which he purchased from William Horsley, in 1781, for £820. He built his Rocester factory in 1782, and the river is thought to have driven two wheels, one external and one internal.

When the mill was up and running it was passed on to his son, Richard Arkwright junior, in 1783. Richard soon sold a third share of the mill to Richard Bridden and in 1806 Bridden acquired full ownership. Bridden died in 1814 and left the mill to his son, Samuel, and in 1825, Francis and John Bridden took over the mill. They struggled to make a success of it, and a Lancashire spinner, Thomas Houldsworth, soon purchased the mill and paid off the mortgage.

Houldsworth certainly made it pay, and he ran it until his death in 1852 when the value of his Manchester and Rocester mills were given as £110,616. The estate was divided among his family and after a number of exchanges, Henry Houldsworth emerged victorious. Under Henry, the mills flourished. He was a true benefactor and he had the village school and workers' cottages built. When he died, in 1868, he left a sound business and a cared for village.

Unfortunately William Henry Houldsworth, his son, was not his father. His tenure was a disaster and the mill closed in 1874. Two years of unemployment tested the resolve of the Rocester cotton workers and it was not until 1876 that they were able to return to work, this time with new bosses, Walter and Charles Lyon who owned the cotton mills at Tutbury. Rocester mill was renamed Tutbury Mill - a strange confusion but one that persisted. The brothers invested a large amount of money in the mill and for the first time in a 1000 years, the waterwheels were abandoned and water turbines installed. The money had to come from somewhere - and by 1900 the company went into voluntary liquidation!

The Churnet Bridge at Rocester with the corn mill to the right.

The cotton mills at Rocester.

Rocester High Street.

Floods at Rocester in the 1960s. *Courtesy of K. Langton*

Fine Spinners Ltd now arrived to become the most consistent of the many owners. They would provide employment for the people of Rocester for over sixty years until they sold out to Courtaulds in 1964, and Courtaulds continued to run the company until the mid-1980s when they finally closed the doors and brought to an end the long association of textiles with the village.

Luckily, for Rocester, other employment was available, the giant complex of JCB had long since replaced the traditional trade as the major employer.

THE BAMFORDS AND JCB

Joseph Cyril Bamford's ancestors were evident in the area around Abbots Bromley, Cotton, Yoxall and Hoar Cross. They were artisans who aspired to yeoman farmers and they went on to establish themselves in agricultural related businesses in Uttoxeter.

In 1844, when Henry Bamford married Julia Brassington at Alton Catholic Church, his father in law installed him in an ironmongery business. The shop was a great success and by 1876 it was described as *'ironmongers and iron-founders'*. From those humble, but fortunate, beginnings the Bamfords expanded into a separate iron foundry in Uttoxeter. The ironmonger's shop became a landmark in Uttoxeter and the iron foundry expanded over several generations to become Bamfords Ltd, designers and manufacturers of agricultural machinery. The quality of their engineering was such that farmers sought out a Bamford machine above all others.

For over a century the company and the family prospered but ultimately, as more family directors and shareholders emerged the company was diluted. Bamfords eventually surrendered to the inevitable in the late 1960s, was taken over briefly, but failed to make a recovery and was closed.

It was into this prosperous and respected family that Joseph was born in 1916. He was the son of Cyril Joseph Bamford and Dolores Turner of The Parks, a fine house on the edge of Uttoxeter. Joe was educated at Stoneyhurst College and joined the family firm in 1935. After serving in the army during the 1939-1945 war, he returned, but tales abound of Joe's dissatisfaction with what he found. Suffice to say that he decided to make his own way in life.

Along the way he married a Uttoxeter girl, Marjorie Griffin, and had two children, Anthony and Mark. Joe became recognised as a world expert on hydraulics and many of his original ideas became accepted as the norm in the field of earth-moving. And among the many factories owned by JCB nowadays is the original Bamford's Leighton Iron Works in Uttoxeter.

After a few false starts, Joe settled into his own business, manufacturing farm trailers in a small lock-up garage in Uttoxeter. From such tiny acorns mighty oak trees grow. In a very short time Joe moved to a farm building in Crakemarsh Hall. Here Joe produced shooting brakes from army surplus vehicles and then began to convert farm tractors into loading shovels. Joe's imagination, and his engineering skills, led to the back hoe and the excavator - the first JCB. It also led him to Rocester as Crakemarsh became too small.

The old farm buildings that Joe now took over have long since been replaced by a modern and much-admired complex that dominates the village. From Rocester, the now famous JCBs are exported all over the world. JCB factories provide employment in other parts of the country. In America a modern manufacturing plant produces excavators for the USA and throughout the world there are JCB distribution and sales centres

Joseph Cyril Bamford died in 2001. The company has been headed by his elder son, Anthony, since Joe retired in 1976.

The prosperity and industry of the town for the best part of 2000 years owes much to the Churnet and its sister river, the Dove. There was also a cheese factory and a brickworks in Rocester, and all the trades that support such a population. One of the owners of the brickworks, situated at Red Hill on Station Road was Mr C.A. Hartley who lived at The Rookery. The Caldon canal also passed through Rocester on its way to Uttoxeter, as did the railway.

The Rookery, home of Mr Hartley, proprietor of Red Hill brickworks. *Courtesy Mrs R. Norton.*

Chapter Twelve
Crakemarsh

A FINE HALL AND FINE FAMILIES

Just a mile or so outside Rocester our journey ends. The Churnet merges with the Dove and the two flow towards the Trent and ultimately the Humber, where traces of the Staffordshire Moorlands are deposited into the North Sea.

The Domesday entry records *'The King holds Crakemers. Earl Alfgar held it. There is half a hide with appendages. There is land for six ploughs. There are 2 villans and 4 bordars with 2 ploughs, and 6 acres of meadow. Woodland 1 league long and as much broad. There is a mill rendering 10s. It is worth 10s.'*

Crakemarsh was small in comparison to the townships of Rocester and Uttoxeter but it was larger than the sprinkling of houses suggest today. The present modern houses occupy a small part of the grounds that was once occupied by Crakemarsh Hall. The eighty seven acres that surrounded the hall have long since passed into private hands.

As for the mill, there is no sign. The Domesday entry simply reminds us again just how important the Churnet was to local industry and how many water mills it supported.

The Crakemarsh estate supported a chapel. The usual practise was to erect a chapel within walking distance of the manor house. Although the site is not precisely marked, we know that in a field called 'Chapel Yard' there is a slightly raised platform that may well have been where the chapel stood. All mention

Crakemarsh Hall

ceased after 1533. The obvious conclusion is that the chapel was built by an occupant of Crakemarsh Hall who was a devout catholic. The date of 1533 is significant enough to suggest that the chapel suffered at the hands of the followers of Henry VIII. There is nothing to suggest that the chapel at Crakemarsh was connected with the monastery at Rocester although Crakemarsh was included in the demesne of the abbey. Croxden abbey also held land around Crakemarsh but again there is nothing that relates to the chapel.

After Alfgar was replaced by the Normans, William I granted the lands to Henry de Ferrers. A descendant, Robert de Ferrers, passed Crakemarsh to his daughter, Maud when she married Bertram de Verdun of Alton. After several generations Crakemarsh passed to Lord Burghersh. From Burghersh it passed to Delves and then to Blounts and so to the Sheffields. Sheffield sold the estate to Gilbert Collier. Collier's son sold it to Sir Gilbert Gerard, Master of the Rolls. From the Gerards it passed to William Cotton about 1658.

A descendant, Elizabeth Cotton married Thomas Sheppard of Bedfordshire in 1774 and in doing so passed on Crakemarsh through the female line. Thomas was created a Baronet in 1809 and on his death in 1821 was succeeded by his son, Thomas Cotton-Sheppard. The Cotton-Sheppards were related through marriage to the Harts of Uttoxeter. Elizabeth Maria Margaret Hart married Richard Cavendish in 1841 and, through a succession of circumstances the Hart-Cavendish family moved into Crakemarsh Hall.

The Cavendish family retained the estate until the death of Tyrell William Cavendish in 1967 when the Crakemarsh estate was put up for sale by auction. The hall was described as a Georgian mansion although it is apparent that an earlier house had existed on the site. The estate was purchased by JCB for £89,000, with the intention of using it for a company training centre. However, the plan was abandoned and the estate sold again in 1976. A fire in 1983 left the hall in ruins and it was demolished - to be purchased for building land.

Crakemarsh made headlines from time to time. During the reign of Edward IV, Sir John Delves enclosed some of the common land used by the people of Uttoxeter who promptly tore down the newly erected hedges. Delves replaced the hedges and left servants in place to guard them. Delves' heir, Sir John Blount, was far more conciliatory and re-opened the enclosure, but Blount's heir, Sir Robert Sheffield, enclosed them once again and in doing so, instigated legal action by the citizens of Uttoxeter in 1502-3.

The Delves may not have been popular around Uttoxeter but they were not lacking in courage. In the Battle of Poitiers, in 1356, Sir John Delves distinguished himself when he *'held the front of the English at Poitiers'*.

Chapter Thirteen
The Churnet Valley Railway

THE BEAUTIFUL RAILWAY

Our journey along the Churnet has taken us a few score miles and through more than 2000 years of history. The many water mills have finished. The closest we can get to the yesterday's technology is the mill of James Brindley in Leek and the twin-wheel flint mill at Cheddleton. Our river worked hard for a living. It powered at least sixteen mills. Corn grinding, flint grinding, colour and dye making, saw pits, wool fulling, forges, smelting and cotton mills.

It may have taken 2000 years for us to arrive but it will not take long for us to get back to Leek. We are going by train and if we hurry we can just catch the 11.15am from Uttoxeter. The journey will take about one and three-quarter hours. If you are thinking that is a long time, remember we have quite a few stations to stop at. From Uttoxeter to Spath and Stramshall, then to Rocester and on to Denstone. From Denstone to Alton, Oakamoor, Kingsley and Froghall, Consall Forge, Cheddleton, Leekbrook and finally, Leek.

While we are travelling we can give some thought to the construction of this wonderful little railway. The forming of the railway was not without controversy. The 1840s heralded a decade of railway mania. Landowners and businessmen alike competed for a piece of the action and several routes were proposed for north and east Staffordshire area. In each and every case a vested interest influenced the decisions of both the government and the investor. The fact that the canal would feel the pinch was not lost on its owners, who fought and later joined the inevitable change.

The carrying capacity and the speed of railways, plus the addition of passenger traffic, gave them an enormous advantage. Just as the canal had replaced the packhorse and the cart, the railways were set to replace the canal. The Caldon Canal Co. accepted the inevitable and promptly joined forces with the railway pioneers. Part of the Caldon canal between Froghall and Uttoxeter was filled in to accommodate the route of the proposed railway from Macclesfield to Uttoxeter, one of several in the area which were intended to link Manchester with Derby, Stafford and Buxton and join the national network.

After a false start, the North Staffordshire Railway, which included the Potteries and the Churnet Valley line, finally made its entrance in 1845/46. The Churnet Valley line was opened on 13th July 1849 and ran from North Rode near Macclesfield to Uttoxeter. Four tunnels were required, one at Leek 462 yards long, one at Birchall 88 yards long, one at Cheddleton 476 yards long and one at Oakamoor 550 yards long - and all still are in existence today. Some of the bridges over the Churnet were of timber construction and remained so until the 1880s, but many well-built brick and stone bridges are still found along the line and its branches.

Uttoxeter was the largest station, incorporating not only the Churnet Valley but also the lines from Stoke-on-Trent, Derby, Stafford and Birmingham. Uttoxeter's popularity was of doubtful benefit in the end to the Churnet Valley line. Although the line retained a steady volume of commercial and passenger traffic, it was easily surpassed by the line from Stoke-on-Trent to Derby which carried up to 50,000 passengers per week and up to 100,000 tons of freight, at least ten times as much as the Churnet.

Not that the sums mattered much to those who used the Churnet Valley line for a hundred years or so as they enjoyed the convenience and the privilege of travelling on one of the most picturesque railways in the country. Travelling to work or to play, for days out or to school, to market or to farm, the line and its branches (including the connection to the narrow gauge Manifold line) were idyllic journeys. The main line ran along the edge of Rudyard Lake, and from Cheddleton followed the beautiful Churnet Valley.

For the most part, the towns themselves remained unaffected by the railway, the old trades and industries remained, and the railway simply replaced canal or road. A few people would travel to distant towns but most were content with their lot and worked locally. The journey changed little as over the intervening years, first the London North Western Railway, and then the London Midland Scottish (LMS), took over the tracks.

We leave Uttoxeter and follow the open pastures along the banks of the Dove and over Spath crossing as it makes its way to Rocester. Rocester was busier than might be expected. Its goods yard received coal, corn, and milk for local distribution, as well as cheese from the nearby factory, and stone from the Hollington quarry. The site also had large grain warehouses for bulk storage and distribution. The Red Hill brickworks was close enough to merit its own side line. In addition, Rocester served as the junction for the line to Ashbourne and Buxton, and the area around the station and the brickworks was a tiny community on the edge of the village - replaced in the 1960s by the JCB works.

Colin Minton Campbell of nearby Woodseat was the chairman of the North Staffs Railway from 1874-1883. He may well have been behind the decision to rebuild Rocester station in 1895. It is said that the Jacobean style of the new station matched its importance as a 'premier' station on the route.

Rocester station.

Rushton station, near to the North Rode end of the Churnet Valley line.

The Land of the Churnet

THE NORTH STAFFORDSHIRE
RAILWAY CO.
- THE 'KNOTTY'.

Leek station.

Denstone, just a mile away, used the Rocester goods yard but retained its own station and stopping point. The Heywoods exerted influence and the halt was built for their convenience as well as the visitors to Denstone College - at times it was busier than Rocester when the College boys were arriving. With its low platform and wooded steps, the ladies could alight with elegance.

We now arrive at Alton station - equally busy at times with visitors to the famous gardens arriving in droves. The Earl of Shrewsbury, not wishing to mix with the masses, had his own waiting room set high above the platform. Across the road, at the lodge entrance to his estate, a luggage lift was installed to take trunks and bags up the incline to the family mansion. Contrary to popular opinion, the station was not designed by Pugin. Its Italianate design is a match of the station at Trentham and is now a listed building.

We know we are approaching Oakamoor station long before we arrive - the pall of smoke hangs over 'Smoakamoor'. It served the Bolton Copper Works and its employees. Sadly it is no longer with us, making way for the car park and picnic area that caters for ramblers and day trippers. But, 'hooray', the Kingsley and Froghall station has recently been rebuilt in the style of the Churnet Valley Railway by the Cheddleton Steam Railway Company.

Although the line from Froghall to Uttoxeter has long since been removed, the track from Froghall to Leekbrook is in regular use, especially during the summer months. The line passes through Consall Forge where the station was opened in 1902 with a clever and efficient use of space, a platform sitting on iron supports above the canal. We alight here for the Black Lion pub, the old iron works and delightful walks through the Consall Country Park.

Onwards to Cheddleton and Basford where the railway station met local agricultural needs in addition to the more substantial ones of the Paper Mills.

At Leekbrook, the station played host to the side line to St. Edwards Hospital as well as the branch line to Waterhouses, Cauldon Lowe and the Manifold Valley. And finally we arrive at Leek, not as busy as Uttoxeter but nevertheless in its day a scene of much hustle and bustle.

Even before Dr Beeching it was evident that the Churnet Valley Line was not paying its way. The branch line from Rocester to Ashbourne and Buxton was the first to close, the last passenger train on 1st November 1954. Fireworks were set off at various stops along the way as people waved a last goodbye. Goods traffic continued for another decade but then ceased in 1964.

On the main line both passenger and freight traffic had been withdrawn by 1964, although a spasmodic service limped along for a few months until 1965 - and as if to mark the end of an era, and to ensure that it would never return, the tracks were uplifted in 1966 to Alton.

GLOSSARY

Some of the words used when the Domesday Book was compiled are no longer in common use but, of necessity, are included in these pages.

BORDAR A cottager or peasant. Of low economic status.

BOVATE One eighth of a carucate.

CARUCATE A ploughland. The area that could be ploughed with an eight ox team.

DEMESNE Land in Lordship whose produce is devoted to the Lord rather than to the tenants.

EARL The chief administrative officer of the king.

FURLONG The length of a furrow. 40 perches. 8 furlongs to a mile

HIDE Standard unit of assessment of tax. The amount of land that would support a household: divided into four virgates.

HUNDRED A sub-division of a Shire with fiscal, judicial and military functions.

LEAGUE In medieval England one league equalled 12 furlongs (8 furlongs = a mile)

MESSUAGE A unit of land comprising a house or houses with appurtenant property.

VILL A village but not in the modern sense. Could also represent an area of land rather than a specific settlement. The lowest unit of administration. Usually covered an inhabited area that would be taxable.

VILLAIN A villager. A peasant of high economic status.

VIRGATE One quarter of a hide.

WASTE Land that did not register dues, usually sparsely inhabited. In some cases, especially in the remote areas of the Churnet Valley, such areas were of industrial enterprise eg iron smelting.

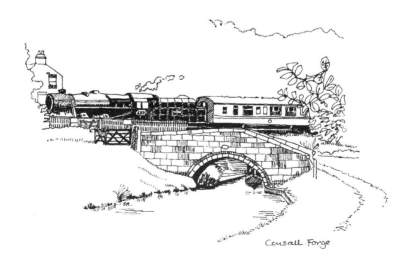

Consall Forge